FREE
TO
SUCCEED

FREE
TO
SUCCEED

12 Dynamic Keys To Experiencing
and Enjoying Godly Success

STEVE DIGGS

B&F

BOYD
&
FRANKLIN
PUBLISHERS

This publication is designed to provide accurate and authoritative information with regard to the subject matter covered. It is made available with the understanding that neither the publisher nor the author is engaged in rendering legal, accounting, investing, or other professional advice. If legal advice or other expert &/or professional assistance is required, the services of a competent professional should be sought. (Developed from a declaration of Principles jointly adopted by a Committee of the American Bar Association and Committee of Publishers and Associations.) You are urged not to act upon any of this material without the advice of a competent professional and/or expert who is also familiar with your individual needs and circumstances.
Please remember that the presenter/author holds a Christian worldview and that all content herein is based upon his understanding of the Bible. Since comments are based on this Christian worldview they may, or may not, always coincide with what is most prudent in strict financial, business, cultural or other terms.

Scripture identified KJV is from the King James Version of the Bible.

Scripture identified NAS is from the New American Standard Bible, © The Lockman Foundation 1960, 1962, 1963, 1968, 1971, 1972, 1973, 1975, 1977.

Scripture identified NIV is from the HOLY BIBLE, NEW INTERNATIONAL VERSION®. NIV®. Copyright, © 1973, 1978, 1984 by International Bible Society. Used by permission of Zondervan Publishing House. All rights reserved.

Scripture identified NKJV is from the New King James Version. Copyright, © 1979, 1980, 1982, Thomas Nelson Publishers, Nashville.

Scripture identified RSV is from the Revised Standard Version of the Bible. Copyright, © 1946, 1952, 1971, 1973 by the Division of Christian Education of the National Council of the Churches of Christ in the United States of America.

To
My parents, Herbert and Verna Diggs,
who taught me to seek
God's will in my life
My wife, Bonnie, who has encouraged
me in the ethics of success
And our herd—
Megan, Joshua, Emilee, and Mary Grace—
whom I hope to never disappoint

Contents

CONTENTS

Acknowledgments

The material between the two covers you are holding represents a lifetime of learning. Among my greatest blessings have been my family, friends, mentors, and teachers who have cared enough to encourage, challenge, and even prod me to strive for excellence. First, I thank my mother and father for teaching me about courage, determination, and principled living. Most of all, I thank them for teaching me about Jesus by living as Jesus lived.

Special thanks to Rubel Shelly, my friend, brother, and encourager. Thanks to the special servants of God who have always been there at crossroad times in my life: Batsell Barrett Baxter, Benny Benjamin, Dave Clayton, Willard Collins, Don Finto, Walt Leaver, Don Loftis, Bob Neil, Bob Oliver, Robert Qualls, and Rod Turnham.

My profound thanks to all of those who proofed this manuscript and offered such valuable advice: my mother and wife, Steve Campbell, Sandra Chaffin, and Alan Bryan. Most of all, gratitude goes to Bob Hendren for helping me maintain correct words and a holy direction.

I express deep appreciation to my secretaries Jennifer Jean and Janet Smith for help on the manuscript. To my administrative assistant, Mitzi Hinton, who went above and beyond the call of duty, thanks a million!

Special thanks to Joshua, Megan, Emilee, and Mary Grace, who allowed their dad time off to work on this book.

Finally, all praise to my God for His full redemption and sweet blessings. I especially thank Him for my wife, Bonnie. She is my advisor, sounding board, and best friend.

---

*"THE BEST AND TRUEST
EVIDENCE OF SUCCESS
IS NOT BASED UPON
WHAT A PERSON OWNS.
IT CAN BE DETERMINED
ONLY BY WHAT A
PERSON IS."*

INTRODUCTION

This book has not been a frivolous undertaking. I have prayed over and pondered its content on many occasions. I am aware that there has been an increasing number of "Christian success" books on the market in the last ten years, and while I don't want to be unduly critical, it worries me that so many of these books are patently non-Christian in their message. Many contain little more than the secular "get all you can grab" mentality that is promoted by the unsaved world. Unfortunately, many Christians have ignored the call upon their lives to be holy in the stampede to be happy. We have listened to false teachers who, by twisting and misapplying Scripture, have convinced us that financial wealth should be our primary goal. What makes this even more insidious is that our great pulpits have often failed to call us back to holiness.

Living in a blessed nation brings with it unique responsibilities. During the Reagan years, many of us were glad to see a greater emphasis on traditional values and morality. Yet we let our collective guard down and bought into a selfish, self-indulgent life-style that is not consistent with the Christian walk. We, in effect, accepted a worldview that is fundamentally non-Christian. Many of us whitewashed orthodox Christian doctrine. We began to believe that good guys always win. We listened to pop psychologists who urged us to "speak" our own reality into existence. We became convinced God had a stockpile of worldly possessions that He dutifully doled out to anyone who paid Him even the slightest lip service.

While my goal in this book is not simply to please men, I must admit that criticism does hurt. I hope I can articulate so as not to be a stumbling block. *Success* is not a bad word. The danger comes in how one defines it. I believe Jesus wants us to enjoy success. However, His definition and the world's definition of *success* are *very* different. In this book, I hope to communicate a spiritual approach that will lead you to His kind of success. Our emphasis will be on success in the business and professional world, but if you are looking for a book that will tell you how to play by the world's rules, this one will disappoint you.

In the coming pages, we will explore some of the traits common to many of the successful people I have known. We will compare the world's approach to, and concept of, success with the way God views success. We will deal with practical problems in the light of our spiritual calling. We'll talk about the issues businesspeople face daily: time pressures, dealing with wealth and greed, people skills, how to manage more effectively and more spiritually. We will search for a biblical perspective on self-confidence, competing aggressively but fairly, and leadership with integrity. My purpose will not be to make an exhaustive study but to hit a number of high points I wish someone had shared with me before I stepped into the world of business. This is a simple, easy-to-read, no-nonsense strategy that outlines the basic steps for understanding and dealing with success from a truly Christian perspective.

Some of the chapters will be basic, how-to lessons. They will cover practical subjects that could well be discussed in a secular book on business technique and etiquette. However, even in these chapters, I hope our focus will be uniquely Christian. The other chapters will be unabashedly spiritual in their content. You may not agree with all of my conclusions. That's okay. If the following pages challenge you to dig deeper into the Word, pray more frequently when making decisions, and long more intensely for an eternal home with God—I will be thrilled!

The Christian community in America is at a crossroads. We can go blithely on, buying into a world system of materialism that bears little resemblance to godly living, or we can redefine success to conform with our Father's view.

Simply stated, our goal will be to learn from God's heart so we can become free to succeed!

To help you or a small group explore in depth the issues raised in this book, please refer to the study questions beginning on page 219.

Free to Succeed

"FOR THE TRUE
FOLLOWER, THE GOAL
IS NOT TO BE HAPPY,
THE GOAL IS TO
BE HOLY."

1

SQUARE PEGS AND ROUND HOLES

There's a story told about a father who gave his little boy a bat and ball for his fifth birthday. The following morning, the little fellow rushed outside to begin practice. All day long he worked at throwing the ball up and trying to hit it.

Finally, about supper time, as his dad pulled into the driveway, Billy rushed up to announce that he'd really mastered this new game of baseball. Excitedly, his dad set his briefcase down and walked around to the backyard to watch his home-grown Babe Ruth.

Sure that he had his father's total attention, Billy threw the ball into the air, cocked the bat, and let it swing. Dad held his breath. *Swoooosh*, went the bat! Alas, the ball hit the ground as the little guy's bat plowed the air.

As his father started to console him, Billy grinned real big, picked up the ball, and said, "That's just strike one."

Again he pitched the ball over his head and swung, the

little bat crashing through space as fast as he could swing it. But again he missed, and the ball fell limply to the ground. Dad said a quick prayer for a hit, tried to camouflage his concern, and sympathized, "That's okay, son, relax. You'll hit the next one."

Billy just smiled at his dad and said, "That was strike two."

Once more he flung the ball up, pulled the bat back, and let it rip. Dad could tell he had a better sight on the ball this time. Billy was holding the bat better, too. Maybe—just maybe. As the ball came down, the bat came around. And by just the slightest margin—Billy missed the ball again.

Unable to hide his sadness, Billy's dad reached out to put his arm around the little set of shoulders, only to look down at the biggest, toothiest grin he'd seen all day. Came the thrilled little boy's squeal, "Isn't it great, Dad—I'm on my way to becoming a major league pitcher!"

A Matter of Perspective

Billy and his dad had two very different perspectives. Often we respond to things based on our perspective. Thus it is with this matter of success. There are two broadly different perspectives on the topic: man's and God's. Simply put, that is what we will be dealing with in this book. We will define *success* by God's standards. Then we'll see how it can be achieved and enjoyed in both our own lives and the lives of those we love and lead.

Frankly, I still have more questions here than answers. The following pages are a reflection of my own struggles. To date, I've dealt with some of these struggles with a degree of success, but in many cases, I'm still in the heat of spiritual battle. However, with God's grace, we will attempt to explore some of these challenges together. Although some of the later chapters will offer practical solutions to daily problems in the workplace (listening skills, time management, goal setting, and so on), our primary focus will be on internal character development rather than technique.

Contrary to what some Christians seem to think, success is not an unholy concept. As a matter of fact, I believe it is a most holy goal, but as I have already suggested, success must first be seen through God's eyes.

God's Unique Plan for Each Person

In his Gospel, the Apostle John tells us that Jesus "knew what was in man" (John 2:25 NAS). Now, apart from the theological points that could be made from this comment, I am impressed by its direct, simple truth. Jesus knows what makes me tick. He really does. It's that simple—and it's that complex! He understands my fears, my problem with pride, my self-doubt, my worry. He clearly understands everything about me. Sometimes I like that. Sometimes I don't.

This brings me to the central point of our focus. God has engineered, designed, and built each one of us with a set of characteristics and abilities that He expects to be used to His glory. Often, we are tempted to pursue our own goals, not God's. The inevitable outcome will be, at best, frustration—at worst, devastation.

All too often, even Christians make plans without seeking God's direction. Then we try to recruit God into the scheme by convincing Him it's a good idea. Yet this is not the way Jesus handled decisions in His own life. Even in His life-and-death struggle in the Garden of Gethsemane, He freely relinquished His will to the Father's will (Luke 22:41–43).

It's a little embarrassing when I realize how much of my

life has been spent trying to cram square pegs into round holes. Possibly my most misguided foray into a realm where I had no business was when I decided to pursue a career in the entertainment field. Seldom has there been such a disproportionate combination of desire and talent. Everything in me wanted to be in show business, yet my family and friends were doing all they could to gently convince me I had barely enough talent to sell the tickets, much less be the star performer.

I wouldn't give up. Through high school and college, I became the "singing scourge" of the Southeast by performing on every stage show and television program that would have me. Whether it was a county fair, a talent show, or a grand opening at a car dealership, I was there, guitar in hand, ready for action. By the time it was all over, I was signed to a major label recording contract, but in my heart of hearts, I knew things weren't right. These minor successes were all hollow. I was pursuing a field in which I had no real gift. Kindly put, my talent was of pygmy proportion. I was like the guy who was singing, "I Left My Heart in San Francisco" when a fellow in the audience stood up to suggest he had left his voice there, too.

Now, if you relate to this sort of frustration, we are fellow strugglers. We both know how it feels (and how bad it hurts) to have dreams that do not coincide with our abilities. We both have felt the depression that comes from such a futile inner conflict.

The good news is that people whose "want to's" and abilities are different often find that their abilities end up leading them to far greater pinnacles of success than they ever dreamed possible. Often, one's eventual success is in an altogether different field than would have previously been expected.

Just Such a Case

A young man named Ed ordered a book to assist him in his study of photography. For weeks he waited for the book's arrival through the mail. Finally, one day a brown-wrapped package came. Excitedly, he rushed to open it, only to be disappointed. Instead of the book on photography, the publisher had mistakenly sent him a book on ventriloquism. Ed almost returned the unwanted book but decided to browse through it first. The time he spent with that book not only changed his life but it also affected the lives of millions of other people. By now, you may have guessed that this was the same Ed who later became known to the world as Edgar Bergen. A generation of people would never have enjoyed the endearing comedy of Charlie McCarthy and Mortimer Snerd if a young Ed Bergen had refused to explore his greater potential.

The point is simple: It is a mistake to try to fill a role that doesn't coincide with your God-given abilities. It has the net effect of making one's life a lie. But many of us spend a lifetime "kicking against the pricks," trying to be something we were never designed to be.

God Doesn't Make Any Appendixes

Now, I know that is kind of an unlikely comment, and until this morning, it had never occurred to me. But the fact is, God doesn't make any appendixes! Let me explain what I mean.

I'm told that the appendix has no apparent reason for being inside the human body. It doesn't help with digestion, circulation, or anything else. It just sort of hangs on to the large intestine and does nothing. The appendix is just there.

When it becomes infected and has to be surgically removed, no one misses it.

God tells us that as Christians, we're all very important. We all have equally critical jobs to perform in the body. They may be different, but they are all vital. In God's economy, there is no place for an appendix. Every part has its job. The elbow joint is vital to overall operations. We have to have big toes to keep our balance. Without fingernails we would itch all the time. Paul develops this analogy further:

> For the body is not one member, but many. If the foot should say, "Because I am not a hand, I am not a part of the body," it is not for this reason any the less a part of the body. And if the ear should say, "Because I am not an eye, I am not a part of the body," it is not for this reason any less a part of the body. If the whole body were an eye, where would the hearing be? If the whole were hearing, where would the sense of smell be? But now God has placed the members, each one of them, in the body, just as He desired. And if they were all one member, where would the body be? But now there are many members, but one body. And the eye cannot say to the hand, "I have no need of you"; or again the head to the feet, "I have no need of you."
>
> 1 Corinthians 12:14–21 NAS

As I grasp more fully the fact that God has a special purpose (function) for me, I'll be more willing to accept His challenges for my life. Knowing that He has my best interests at heart will make it easier for me to trust Him. I'll be less afraid of stepping out of the boat.

Stepping out in a new and different direction can be scary. Getting out of our comfort zone usually means change. It takes guts to reevaluate and alter the track one has been following. It can be frightening to leave the security of the "tried and true" and strike out in a new direction, but that's just the way life is. In all the years I have played and watched the game of baseball, I've never seen anyone steal second base without first taking his foot off first.

Doing It God's Way

Granted, God's teachings in Scripture are absolute. He means business. No individual has the right to pick and choose which commands of God he will follow. For instance, I cannot please God if I agree to refrain from being a drunkard yet decide to be a liar. There are certain absolutes all Christians must subscribe to if we are to walk righteously before God. However, within this broad framework all serious Christians must live by, I believe God works with each one of us individually. Now I know some people have a hard time buying into this, yet we readily accept the obvious fact that God has made each of us physically different. Why, then, do we find it so hard to believe He has built within each of us different emotions, attitudes, and abilities, as well? If we will only let Him, God will play out His will in each individual's life in a beautifully unique way—as unique as our fingerprints.

But for God to do this, we must willingly allow Him into the daily affairs of our lives. For the earnest Christian, there is no such thing as "Sunday-only religion." We cannot compartmentalize God. He wants to be involved in every aspect of our endeavors. God is not available on an a la carte basis. We must let God live and move freely in the daily course of our lives. We should apply His principles to every important decision. We need to solicit His biblical advice as we chart the direction of our lives. To paraphrase the popular lyric, "Unless God is Lord *of* all—He's not Lord *at* all."

To Feel the Pleasure of God

I am an admirer of Eric Liddell, the celebrated track star who represented Great Britain in the Olympic Games of 1924 in Paris, France. Despite numerous obstacles, he became a gold medalist that year. Liddell made a comment that has become very significant to me. He said, "When I am running, I feel the pleasure of God."

What a thought: to *feel* the pleasure of God! Yet much of humanity lives and dies without that achievement, and isn't that a shame? So many of us go through life resolved to do things our own way, as if "our way" would of necessity ensure happiness and success.

There was a popular song a few years back in which the singer bragged that he had always done things his way. He fought everyone who stood in his way and dominated his surroundings. I would submit that this individual had missed the most basic element of success. Doing things our way very rarely brings true, sustainable happiness, and without a Christ-centered happiness and contentment, true success can never be a reality in one's life.

So how does one find the kind of success that leads to true happiness? According to many of today's self-help books, it is simple. You merely assert yourself. You make sure you outtalk, outdazzle, outsell, and outpitch the other guy. At first you try manipulative gentility. If that doesn't achieve the desired results, you put on a pair of cleats and run over him. After all, goes the argument, all that matters is the bottom line.

The Better Way

Far too many people in our society are convinced that the correct spelling for *success* is "$uccess." While some successful people do have financial wealth, money is not a measure of true success. As a matter of fact, some people who have spent a lifetime striving to become wealthy are now finding it doesn't even bring the prestige they had expected. According to an article in the December 17, 1990, issue of *Fortune* magazine, conspicuous consumption is no longer the vogue:

> David Meer, a senior vice president of DYG Inc., a consumer-research and consulting firm, said, ". . . the Nineties will see a marked change in the way society defines success, with achievements such as a happy family life and service to one's community replacing money as the measure of one's worth. We see it as the search for happiness in a post-affluent society."

This point was brought home to me in a very forceful way not long ago when my son, Joshua, and I took a three-day trip in Ensenada, Mexico, to visit an orphanage our church supports. The director at The City of Children is a glowing man named Stan Stout. He's also tough-minded and determined. But most of all, he loves the Lord. During our visit, Stan told me about some of the hardships they have to endure: dirty water, a constant need for funds, sad cases of children who were abused by their families. I also learned a good deal about Stan and his wife, Carole.

Before coming to work at The City of Children, Stan had been an unusually successful stockbroker and investment banker. Stan had traveled in the best of circles. He knew all the important players. He and Carole had owned a beautiful, thirty-five-hundred-square-foot home in Southern California. They spent free time on their boat. With an annual income in the hundreds of thousands of dollars, they had no financial worries.

"Why," I asked, "did you give all that up to do this?"

Stan chuckled and said, "Steve, I didn't give up anything except a lot of striving and struggling for things that really weren't important. I was spending most of my time building financial wealth and missing out on the blessings that come from building eternal wealth. Take a look around you—these kids love me and I love them. Now, you tell me if that's not true wealth!"

Isn't it wonderful how God's plan for success frees us to serve Christ and those He created? It's only through such a servant mentality that we will really become free to succeed.

The Way of the World

The fact is, the humanistic approach to success isn't new. It has always been with us. We live in a fallen, hurting world. People who don't know Jesus are like blind men trapped in a burning building. They scramble feverishly to find a way out of their misery. Running into walls, they fall down basement stairways in a frantic search for release. So it is for the man or woman who attempts to succeed without first knowing God. Some look for answers in drugs; some in illicit relationships; some with an undue love for money and prosperity. Society seems convinced that an individual is a success in life when all he has made is money. You may have seen the bumper sticker that communicates this worldly concept beautifully. It says, "Whoever dies with the most toys— wins."

Back in 1923, a group of the world's most successful financiers got together at a Chicago hotel. Included were the presidents of a leading steel manufacturer, the largest utility company, the New York Stock Exchange, and the Bank of International Settlements. There was even a member of the President's cabinet present. Over the years, magazines and newspapers had printed the various success stories of these tycoons, urging young people to follow their example. It was no wonder. Collectively, these guys controlled more wealth than there was in the United States Treasury!

However, only twenty-five years later, things had really changed. Charles Schwab, the great steel magnate, spent the last five years of his life living on borrowed money—and died penniless. Richard Whitney, president of the New York Stock Exchange, had recently been released from prison. Albert Fall, the member of the President's cabinet, was pardoned from prison so he could die at home. Leon Fraser, president of the Bank of International Settlement, committed suicide. Ivar Kreuger, head of the world's greatest monopoly, also killed himself.

All of these men had learned how to make money, but not a single one of them had learned to live successfully. Still, today's business barons tell us that money and power indicate how well we're doing on the "Successometer." Success, they tell us, is essentially a game of Monopoly played in the real world.

Grabbing the Brass Ring

There is one small problem with all of this: It doesn't square with what God says success is all about. I've spent a number of years watching all types of people grab for what they thought was the brass ring of success. Most have yet to even touch it. Others have grabbed hold and briefly held on, only to drop it forthwith. Then there is that small minority of people who have grabbed the brass ring of success and really managed to hold on to it.

This small group of people usually look the same as others around them, and contrary to popular belief, they are not necessarily any brighter than their peers. But there is something very different about them.

They approach life with a different attitude from other people. Instead of worrying about grabbing the brass ring for themselves, they are more likely to be lifting other people up to the brass ring. Frequently, their peers will describe them with phrases such as, "He really seems to know what counts," or, "She sure seems to know what really matters in life."

The obvious question is, "What do these folks know that I don't know, and how can I learn it?"

As a beginning point, let's simply admit the obvious: We all want to experience success. However, for most of us, this seemingly simple goal has been the greatest challenge of our lives.

Before you progress further in this book, realize two things: (1) God longs for you to experience *His* kind of success, and (2) while our goals may vary, the ingredients of success are somewhat universal and very attainable.

In the upcoming pages, we are going to define *success* by God's standards. We'll take this elusive commodity off the shelf. We'll examine it from a number of different directions. Then, we'll attempt to plan a strategy for getting from where we are to where we want to be.

The desire to be successful is not an unholy goal. However, we must understand *success* by God's definition. To this end, God has blessed each of us with a unique set of abilities that He expects us to use to His glory—not our own. As an individual learns what his or her abilities are and begins using them, the stage is set for God to play out His will in that person's life.

"SUCCESS LIES NOT IN
ACHIEVING WHAT YOU
AIM AT BUT IN AIMING AT
WHAT YOU OUGHT
TO ACHIEVE."
—AUTHOR UNKNOWN

TWO GREAT SECRETS OF SUCCESSFUL PEOPLE

In this chapter, I want to share with you what I believe are two great secrets of achieving and maintaining the type of success God would have for us. But first, let's take a moment to define what *true success* is and what it is not. For anything of value, there will always be counterfeits and copies. Success is no different. There is always an abundance of hucksters and hustlers with their "money-back guarantee" success formulas. As we will see, our society equates success with money, power, and sexual conquests.

After the death of one of Hollywood's stars, columnist Rona Barrett was asked the question, "Do you know any other superstars in the world of entertainment or sports who might also be in danger of taking their lives?" Barrett answered, "I don't know of any who are not in danger of either deliberately or accidentally taking their own lives, because I don't know a single one who is really happy." What a sad commentary. Among those people most of the world would consider at the pinnacle of success, such alarming despair! They have wealth, everywhere they go people recognize them and ask for autographs, many travel with doting entourages that tend to every real and perceived need. Yet in spite of having everything under the sun, true happiness eludes them. There must be something more!

As I have already suggested, if success and godly happiness are not the same thing, they are at least so closely interwoven that one cannot exist without the other. To suggest that either success or happiness can exist without the other is like suggesting that a person can tie shoes that have only one lace. Accordingly, the idea that stockpiling material possessions will, of necessity, assure happiness makes no sense. After surveying all of the wealth, power, and prestige the world had to offer, King Solomon realized just how empty and vain it all was:

> Thus I considered all my activities which my hands had done and the labor which I had exerted, and behold all was vanity and striving after the wind and there was no profit under the sun.
>
> Ecclesiastes 2:11 NAS

The fact is, Jesus wants us to know His kind of happiness. The Beatitudes (Matthew 5:1–12) tell us how to develop happiness, or success, in our individual lives. As we acquire these traits, we will become more like Jesus and less like the world.

The First Secret . . .

So, what are the two great secrets of success? First, we must begin believing a couple of things about God: He knows the ingredients of real happiness and success, and He wants us to enjoy real happiness and success. Sounds simple enough. Right? Wrong. No matter how simply God lays out the game rules, we seem driven to find a different rule book. We want to complicate things. We want to restructure things so they make better sense to us. We just aren't quite convinced that the same God who drew up the original plans and built us knows how to maintain us at peak performance.

God's formula for success is somewhat different from man's. Man says, "Push and promote yourself to the front." Jesus tells us that success comes when we do not strive to be the most prominent. In Luke 14, He tells us that if we take a seat at the head table at a banquet, we may be embarrassed when the host asks us to move to allow room for a more distinguished guest. Instead, Jesus says, we should take the least important seat. Then, when the host invites us to move up higher, we will have honor in the sight of all.

Now, wait just a minute! There's something inside me that says this is inherently wrong. It's backwards. If I want to be a success, I'd better be sure I'm at the front of the line. It all may be good in theory, but this isn't the way success is achieved in today's world. Maybe that's the way it was accomplished two thousand years ago when people rode donkeys, slept on dirt floors, and thought a juggler in the marketplace was big-time entertainment, but here in the last decade of the twentieth century, things are different. It's a more competitive world today.

Hit songs are filled with lyrics such as, "Only strong people survive." Ruthless business magnates who have clawed their way to the top (often leaving scores of bloodied bodies behind) get big advances to publish their primal techniques in "how to" books. Business magazines flourish with bold cover stories that glorify the most ferocious captains of the business world. Just how sure can we be that God really still has a handle on what it takes to succeed in today's world? Isn't it possible that the rules of the game have changed over the years? Besides, who says good guys will always come out ahead in the end? I'm just not that sure I want to wear a white hat!

We must remind ourselves again what success is—and what it is not. If we confuse ultimate success with a big office, designer clothes, a two-Jacuzzi home, and an Italian sports car that sneers instead of purrs, God's approach will seem senseless. But if we remember that all-important link between success and happiness, God's way to success holds validity.

One doesn't have to look far beyond today's headlines to be overwhelmed by the number of people the world would describe as successful whose lives are in a shambles. These are the very people who seemingly have it all. We read about them in newspapers and business magazines. They speak to graduate students in leading business schools. We see them on television with Phil and Oprah. Whether it is a dynamic young presidential hopeful who destroys his career through sexual indiscretions, a Fortune 500 business leader whose third marriage is on the rocks, or a highly paid star athlete who ends up in prison because of drug-related problems, we don't have to exaggerate the facts to convince any fair-minded person that this world's idea of success leaves a lot to be desired.

Filling the Hole in Our Heart

We each have a hole in our heart. Most people spend an entire lifetime trying to fill up that hole. Some try to fill it with possessions, some with power and prestige, many with sexual conquests. Others eventually despair and try to fill their heart holes with drugs and alcohol. Unfortunately, very few people ever stop to examine the hole itself. Those few who do study the hole gain an important insight into filling it, because as they contemplate the hole, they realize it is shaped like Jesus—and nothing else will ever adequately fill it.

When all is said and done, maybe God's timeless approach to finding success really does hold merit. Maybe God wasn't playing a cruel joke on the human race when He said that if we want to experience genuine happiness and success, we will make it a point to love and pray for our rivals (Matthew 5:44). Jesus said that before we will be prepared to receive His blessings, we must be willing to give to those who are in need (Luke 6:38, 12:33).

He also taught that successful people don't always make the most "career oriented" decisions. In Luke 14:12–14 NAS, we are told that successful people don't always associate with other successful people:

> And He also went on to say to the one who had invited Him, "When you give a luncheon or a dinner, do not invite your friends or your brothers or your relatives or rich neighbors, lest they also invite you in return, and repayment come to you. But when you give a reception, invite the poor, the crippled, the lame, the blind, and you will be blessed, since they do not have the means to repay you; for you will be repaid at the resurrection of the righteous."

There are times when the truly successful person invests time (and money) in those who cannot afford to return his or her hospitality.

Jesus Practiced What He Preached

Now, I don't know about you, but I don't put a lot of stock in someone's teaching until I am convinced that the individual has followed his own advice and has succeeded in doing so.

This brings me to the most convincing proof of all that God's formula for success is legitimate: God followed it Himself! You see, God in His infinite love and knowledge knew that the only way He would ever find true happiness would be by drawing all people unto Himself. For whatever reason, God really wanted to have fellowship with us. He is happy only when we have become members of His family. Since man had absolutely no way of saving himself, God's only alternative was to give sinful man the greatest gift of all: His own Son. Jesus, the King of Kings, came to earth as a Servant and found happiness by giving Himself up to be murdered. Through this sacrifice, God's heart is made happy by every sinner who accepts this free gift of salvation.

The Second Secret . . .

The second great secret of success is to learn to listen when God is talking to us. Whoops! Was that someone's jaw I just heard drop? Am I suggesting that we can expect to hear God talk to us today in an audible way? As much as I wish I could say yes to this question, my experience has never included such a conversation with God.

However, I am convinced that God speaks to His people today in three ways. The first way is through His written Word, the Bible. Trying to succeed before God without being an avid student of the Bible is like trying to build a skyscraper without unrolling the blueprint—it can't be done!

One Man's Success Story

I have always been a student of successful people. One of the people I admire most is Alton Howard. We first met in the mid-1980s when he hired our advertising/public relations firm to help with one of his projects. Until then, I had only known this Louisiana businessman by reputation. Alton was into everything from oil drilling to retailing and from publishing to video production. The thing that impressed me most was his reputation as a generous, godly man. Alton has the distinction of being omnisuccessful. In addition to material blessings, he has a beautiful marriage, devout children, friends all over the world, and a beautiful, Christlike peace.

When Alton Howard invited me to be an overnight guest in his home one night in 1985, I was understandably eager. As the car pulled up to his home, I was impressed by its size and elegance. What would I find inside such a lovely residence? What secrets of success would I learn during this visit? Maybe he would have a special planning room where he mapped out his strategies. Maybe he would have motivational plaques on the walls. Maybe he would have a computerized stock market system.

Today, years later, the thing I remember most is what I saw next to Alton's personal reading chair. On the table next to his chair was biblical literature with the obvious signs of having been recently read.

Alton understood that one of the most important trips any of us will ever take is only sixteen inches long. It's the trip that the information in our minds takes down into our hearts. You see, a person becomes what he reads, studies, and thinks about, so if we are in agreement that God is the Author of true success, it follows that those desiring to gain success will spend time reading God's Word and related books.

The second way God speaks to us today is through other people. Often we can learn a lot (and avoid a tremendous amount of failure and heartache) if we are willing to listen and learn from more mature Christians. If I had a dollar for every time God has led my path to cross that of another Christian just when I needed advice most, I would be able to wallpaper my office with money!

Obviously, one must filter any advice he gets through the screen of God's Word. If you listen to everyone who chooses to make you a dumping ground for their particular brand of wisdom, you will drown in an ocean of verbal confusion. However, Proverbs 11:14 kjv gets right to the point when it reminds us, "Where no counsel is, the people fall: but in the multitude of counsellors there is safety."

The Five-Minute Message

If I had only five minutes to spend advising a young person on how to succeed, one of my first suggestions would be to find at least one or two mature Christian mentors. Ideally, these should be older individuals who have had lots of "real world" experience yet have remained utterly faithful to the Lord. They should be people who are intimately acquainted with God and committed to prayer. Additionally, these should be people with whom you can build a real, gut-level rapport. Study the way they deal with their daily challenges. Ask lots of questions. Then do a lot of listening. You would be wise to seek their counsel and advice before making major decisions that will have long-term impact.

I believe a third way we hear God is through circumstance. Again, if not cautiously monitored, we can be confused and misled by assuming that every event in our lives has some spiritual significance. Through the ages, there have always been people who have associated a godly message with every rainfall, job offer, and other occurrence in life. This is not only foolish, it can also lead to all sorts of failed efforts and even to eventual cynicism concerning the basics of an individual's walk with God.

Recently, I received an urgent phone call from a Christian businesswoman whom I had only known casually. She asked me if we could meet to discuss a personal concern she was dealing with. We agreed on a time later that afternoon.

When she arrived at my office, it was obvious there was a problem. As soon as we were seated, she began telling me of a failed business venture that had involved the purchase of an out-of-town radio station. Because of some incorrect assumptions and questionable claims on the part of others, this woman had lost many thousands of dollars. In the end, she had lost the station, too.

She told me how she had prayed and asked God for guidance before making the purchase. She thought it was God who had opened the doors to make the purchase possible. When the station failed, she was mystified. As we continued to talk, she made a comment I could really relate to. She said, "Maybe I thought it was God's will because I *wanted* it to be His will. I'm now afraid that I ran ahead of God. Maybe I was kicking the doors down instead of waiting for God to open them."

Boy, could I connect with that! There have been so many times in my life when I've charged ahead and God wasn't really in it. I am a world-class door kicker. All too often, I've pushed ahead to my own detriment before seeking God's will. We must seek God's direction very carefully and quietly. It is so easy to squelch the Spirit and miss God's message. We won't hear God's direction clearly until we put our own will and ambition on hold. We have to be prepared to accept God's will, no matter what it is. It involves a heart-level response to God that says, "Defeat me if this is not Your way." Then, and only then, do we offer God a heart He can work with.

God does respond to a believer who prayerfully seeks His

direction. I believe God frequently answers the prayer for direction and wisdom by opening the appropriate doors of opportunity and then confirming it in the Christian's mind with a calm, assured peace. In 1 Corinthians 2:10–15, Paul talks about this inner awareness that comes from the Spirit of God. In verses 12 and 13 NAS, Paul says, "Now we have received, not the spirit of the world, but the Spirit who is from God, that we might know the things freely given to us by God, which things we also speak, not in words taught by human wisdom, but in those taught by the Spirit, combining spiritual thoughts with spiritual words."

In his commentary on Corinthians, William Barclay talks about the importance of the Holy Spirit's relationship to God and His function in building up the Christian:

> Paul lays down the fundamental truth that the only person who can tell us about God is the Spirit of God. He uses a human analogy. There are certain things which only a man's own spirit knows. There are feelings which are so personal, things which are so private, experiences which are so intimate that no one knows them except a man's own spirit. No one can really see into our hearts and know what is there except our own spirits. Now, Paul goes on to argue, the same is true of God. There are deep and intimate things in God which only God's Spirit knows; and that Spirit is the only person who can lead us into really intimate knowledge of God. There are things that the unaided power of thought would never find out; the Spirit has to teach them to us for the Spirit alone knows them.

KEY #2

The two secrets of true success are: (1) realizing that God knows the ingredients of success and is willing to share them with us, and (2) being ready to listen when God speaks.

Whether we realize it or not, God's approach is the only surefire plan for happiness and success. There is no other way. We need to understand that God knows what each one of us requires for success, and He wants to see us arrive at His form of success.

This means playing by God's rules. It means pursuing success differently from the way most people do. It involves becoming less so we can be more. It means serving the needs of others before our own. It requires becoming a servant in order to be a better leader. In a word, it means becoming more like Jesus every day. (We will talk more about servanthood leadership in chapter 6.)

As we relinquish our rights to God, He will draw us closer and closer to His heart. God's goals will become our goals. Things that make God happy will make us happy. God will bless our study of His Word and the counsel we seek from other Christians. He will lovingly hear and answer our prayers for direction and guidance. He will become our Senior Partner. If our hearts are open to His direction, He will lead us to a form of success that is success indeed.

"*EVEN YOUTHS GROW
TIRED AND WEARY, AND
YOUNG MEN STUMBLE AND
FALL; BUT THOSE WHO
HOPE IN THE LORD WILL
RENEW THEIR STRENGTH.
THEY WILL SOAR ON WINGS
LIKE EAGLES; THEY WILL
RUN AND NOT GROW WEARY,
THEY WILL WALK AND NOT
BE FAINT.*"
—ISAIAH 40:30, 31 NIV

3

RACING WITH
THE RATS

When an individual makes up his or her mind to accomplish anything worthwhile, there will always be opposition. When one person in an organization awakens to the possibilities of a better future, there will always be those prepared to explain why it can't be done. When an individual dares to try and improve the status quo, there will certainly be those who will assign impure motives to that individual. For every good idea, there are fifty people with reasons it won't work. The greatest enemy of success isn't your competitor; it's a friend who doesn't believe you can pull it off.

The Bible is full of such examples. Do you recall the story of David and Goliath? The biggest hurdle for David to get over wasn't the Philistine with a pituitary problem. It was his own brother and King Saul! Let's pick up the biblical account with the response of David's oldest brother, Eliab:

. . . Eliab's anger burned against David and he said, "Why have you come down? And with whom have you left those few sheep in the wilderness? I know your insolence and the wickedness of your heart; for you have come down in order to see the battle." . . . Then Saul said to David, "You are not able to go against this Philistine to fight him; for you are but a youth while he has been a warrior from his youth."

1 Samuel 17:28, 33 NAS

And who will ever forget Job's wife's words of understanding and encouragement when he was experiencing tough times? When poor Job was at his lowest, she shared these words of comfort: "Do you still hold fast your integrity? Curse God and die!" (Job 2:9 NAS).

Possibly the most penetrating illustration in Scripture of someone's small thinking is recorded in Matthew 16:21–23 when Jesus attempts to tell His disciples about the coming suffering and crucifixion. Here we see Peter taking Jesus aside to rebuke Him and tell Him this will never happen. Instead of taking comfort in Peter's comments, Jesus sees clearly what is happening. Listen to His insightful and vigorous response in verse 23 NAS: "Get behind Me, Satan! You are a stumbling block to Me; for you are not setting your mind on God's interests, but man's."

A Fire and the Lives It Changed

The summer of 1871 was an unusually dry one in Chicago. The rainfall was only a fourth the normal amount. Throughout the city, wooden buildings stood like kindling. Late in the day of October 8, a fire broke out in Mrs. Patrick O'Leary's barn on the Southwest Side. Racing north and east through the city, the flames killed at least three hundred people and destroyed $200 million in property.

Dozens of store owners watched their businesses go up in flames. For many, it was too much to take. The charred ruins of their former stores caused some to give up totally. Others moved away and started other companies that would never again compare with the businesses they had lost. But one thirty-seven-year-old man who had lost his store chose not to listen to the negativity. From the rubble of his burned store, he dared to dream of a vast new merchandising empire that would be built on the same site. It was Marshall Field's dream that became the retailing chain which bears his name to this day.

Insulated, Not Isolated

To survive in a negative world, you have to live above the small thinking that surrounds you. You have to run with the other rats without becoming a victim of the rat race. In other words, although you may have to live and work with short-sighted people, you don't have to buy into their shortsightedness.

Jesus realized this danger. He wanted His disciples to be involved in others' lives without becoming partakers in their sins. Today, He expects His followers to be the visionaries in their societies. Christians, more than any other group, should be able to see the greater potential. Only moments before His betrayal, Christ prayed that His apostles would keep their focus:

> I have given them Thy word; and the world has hated them, because they are not of the world, even as I am not of the world. I do not ask Thee to take them out of the

world, but to keep them from the evil one. They are not of
the world, even as I am not of the world. Sanctify them in
the truth; Thy word is truth. As Thou didst send Me into
the world, I also have sent them into the world.

John 17:14–18 NAS

Jesus was praying that His apostles would be *insulated*, not
isolated, from the world. He knew it would be easy for them
to piously isolate themselves from hurting people. In the
story of the Transfiguration (Matthew 17:1–9), it appears that
even Peter may have had a weakness in this direction. He
had enjoyed that mountaintop spiritual experience so much,
he didn't want to return to the people in the valley below. As
long as he was on the mountain, there weren't any hungry
beggars, abused children, or people with open sores. On top
of that mountain everything was just right—no problems.
Peter asked Jesus for permission to spend more time on the
mountain. He even suggested taking time to build three al-
tars! Yet despite Peter's request, Jesus knew it was time to
return to the task.

I have so many shortcomings. I am frequently disappointed in my wife's husband. I hate to admit it, but there is
a lot of Peter's nature in me. It is so easy to look the other
way when I see a need. I always have a good reason not to
become involved: "I'll be late for an appointment," "Someone else will come by," or the ever popular, "I don't have
time to stop, I'll be late for church."

What frightens me the most is that these excuses for not
becoming involved are very close to the excuses used by the
priest and the Levite who ignored the man who was beaten
and left to die beside the road. This parable in Luke 10:25–37
leaves little doubt as to who the hero really was. It was the
Samaritan, who had the necessary vision to look past the

man's nationality and see his needs. Three men were given the opportunity to become involved. Only one man had the vision to do so, and only one man received the blessing for doing so.

Jesus always taught against isolation and withdrawal. He doesn't want Christians to have a defeated, pessimistic outlook. Sure, mankind is riddled with sin and evil. We live in a fallen world. But as Christians, we have the answer! Jesus wants us to be alive and involved. In Matthew 5:13, He reminds followers that we are the salt of the earth. As they say, "Salt ain't no good until it gets out of the shaker."

While Jesus did not want the Father to take Christians out of the world, He did want us to be insulated from the evil one. In Ephesians 6:10–18, we are told that God's insulation from a sinful world comes by putting on the full armor of God and through prayer.

Insulated from the devil's schemes but not isolated from hurting people. Now that's a neat concept. Coincidentally, it is the same concept that is needed to succeed in any other realm.

In order to succeed, we must deal with other people. We have to be involved in their lives. We have to respond to their needs and concerns. But we must never allow other people to direct and determine our attitudes. The goal: to be insulated from their pessimism and negativism but never isolated from them as people.

Negative thinking is an inescapable cancer of society. It has always been here. It always will be here. Even people of high standing are plagued with this disease. In 1899, Charles Duell, commissioner of the United States Patent Office, urged President McKinley to abolish the patent office. His reason? He was convinced that everything that could be invented had been invented.

Part of the Christian calling involves having an overall optimism in our outlook. Jesus gets a lot of bad press because of people who profess to be Christians but are just as negative as their lost friends. To be brutally graphic, a Christian should not be the one who looks at a truckload of coffins and worries that his may be on board. After all, for a Christian, the grave holds no real dread.

Getting Above the Maze

Now, back to our little rat race analogy. You may remember seeing a rat maze experiment in a college psychology class. That's the experiment where they put a rat into a box filled with walls and partitions just high enough so the rodent can't see over the top. The rat's job is to find the correct path and maneuver through the puzzle from one end to the other. If he does everything just right, there will be a piece of cheese at the end of his trip. Now, this can be a tough task for a little guy with an IQ that starts with a decimal point.

It's too bad there is no way he can get a sky view of the maze. If somehow he could look down at the maze from up above, his job would be a cinch, but he can't do that. So, our little buddy bumps his nose through a trial-and-error existence. What a depressing way to live!

Many of us live our lives the same way. We are constantly in a maze of negative thinking and confident defeatism. We know there are successful people out there, and sure, we would enjoy their life-style. But deep inside, we feel it will never happen for us. All we can see on every side is another wall, so we, too, live lives filled with bruised noses and dashed hopes. We are in a maze of negative thoughts and attitudes. We forget that as Christians we have the power to live above this. No matter how rough it gets, we have the promise that one day God will wipe away all of our tears.

Our first impulse may be to try and escape the maze, but this really is no solution. That would be isolation or withdrawal. God's successful people haven't broken out of their mazes. Their lives are filled with all the problems and challenges other folks experience. So what makes them different? They have simply learned to live and thrive within their mazes. The solution is to work within our limitations, yet find a servant-hearted, abundant life-style.

Few of us ever realize that, unlike the rat, we *can* get a sky view that makes sense of our mazes. As Christians, we have a God in heaven who not only has a sky view but also wants to give us a road map with the best route already marked! He wants us to find the kind of true success that comes only from relinquishing our will totally to Jesus' call upon our lives.

Not realizing this, many people never understand that God wants them to enjoy His best in their lives. Often, they spend a lifetime blaming others for their failures. Their early years in business are spent in hostile rivalries, and their latter years are bitter and cynical. They never realize that their problem is between their own two ears!

Capturing the Uncommon Vision

To persevere in difficult circumstances, a person has to have an uncommon vision. As we've seen, success doesn't always come to the brightest, or the prettiest, or the best connected. It often comes to that individual who keeps on keeping on, doing the same right things, over and over again. It comes to the person who holds more tightly to Jesus' hand with each discouragement. Ultimately, victory comes to the person who gets up just one more time than he falls down.

Now, if this is starting to sound like another one of those "pull yourself up by your own bootstraps" books, read a little farther.

This is where I differ with so much of the humanistic stuff that is being peddled today. It is popular to tell would-be success stories that all they have to do is think positive. People are being told that success is a matter of attitude. All you have to do, they say, is, "Fake it until you make it." Granted, there is an element of truth to all this. One has to dream big and think big to see big accomplishments, and as we've said, without the right mental attitude, mastery usually never comes. Throughout this book, I want to challenge you to work for that right mental attitude. Positive thinking is a real and legitimate trait of any successful person. Your achievements will never exceed your dreams and goals.

It is easy to miss the whole point if we don't approach achieving success from God's perspective. To enjoy the kind of success God wants for us, we need to have His viewpoint on two key issues: First, we must know and accept God's concept of success. Second, we need to clearly understand our position before God. Let's explore God's heart on these two matters.

The God Facade

Many Christians spend their lives striving for a type of success that is in conflict with God's purpose for them. Again, remember that there is a difference between God's definition of *success* and the world's definition. The secularists tell us success can be measured by our net worth. God sees it differently. As we've seen, God equates our success with our level of discipleship.

This brings me to a very timely matter. There is a heresy in Christendom today that may be every bit as dangerous as the Gnostic heresy of the second century. I alluded to this false doctrine earlier. Now I want to be more explicit. Like any other false teaching, it contains just enough truth to sound plausible to the casual hearer, and like many heresies, it is being spread by naive Christians.

I'm referring to the "Health, Wealth, and Prosperity" pitch. Others have dubbed it the "Name It and Claim It" and the "Blab It and Grab It" belief. Whichever title you apply, it is coming from far too many of our preachers and teachers today. No doubt you have heard it on radio or read it in various books. It has become the pop Christianity of our age.

Although the miscellaneous claims and promises vary, the root message is always the same: If you are a Christian, God is duty-bound to make your stay on this planet an appetizer for heaven. Usually the guy's line includes a promise of good health and all the money you want. He may follow that with a worn-out phrase like, "God didn't put all the good things on this earth for the devil's kids to enjoy." Then the speaker usually distorts a couple of Scriptures so they support his premise, gets the audience cheering at a fever pitch, and asks for a contribution. Now, if I sound too cynical, please forgive me, but this teaching makes my blood boil.

I call it the "God Facade" because it counterfeits the Christian ethic. This false belief has allowed Christians to become greedy and materialistic with no sense of guilt or remorse. It promotes the idea that, instead of being servants, we are here to be served by God Himself! It teaches that God somehow owes us whatever we ask Him for. The strong implication is that true followers will receive a lot of loot, and if for some reason we experience defeat, it's a sure sign that our walk with God is lacking.

Only in America

When you get right down to it, this is probably one of the most culturalized heresies ever to hit Christendom. This is an Americanized form of Christianity that would be scorned in nearly every other nation of the world. Just think of the response one of its proponents would get in famine-ravaged Ethiopia or Communist China!

Our family is personally involved in a preachers' training school in Honduras. I try to make a short trip down to the facility about once a year. My visits have taught me two things about the Christians in that part of Central America: (1) They are totally dedicated to serving God—they *really* know Him, and (2) these dear people are desperately poor.

On our last trip, we visited a family of four wonderful people. The parents, both devout Christians, had two small children. The father was studying to preach the Gospel. They planned to return to their home in El Salvador after graduation and start a church. However, the entire family was living in one room that was approximately ten square feet in size. All four slept on a single mattress that lay on the floor. They shared a primitive bathroom with several other families and cooked their meals on hot plates. How dare someone suggest that these good people were living in poverty because of sins in their lives!

Even the Apostle Paul reminds us that "there were not many wise according to the flesh, not many mighty, not many noble" who came to know Jesus (1 Corinthians 1:26 NAS). Paul's comment here sure doesn't sound like one of the modern-day recruiting pitches we hear.

Three Problems With This Teaching

The "Name It and Claim It" teaching does a disservice to everyone. First, it encourages a false sense of security by telling people that wealth is a certain sign of God's favor. There is nothing new about this teaching. Even the Jews of Jesus' day thought rich people were closer to God. This is evidenced in the story of the rich young ruler who came to Christ for advice (Matthew 19:16–26). After he had rejected the Lord's direction for his life and left in sorrow, Jesus commented on how difficult it is for the rich to enter the kingdom of heaven. Verse 25 NAS makes an interesting statement: "And when the disciples heard this, they were very astonished and said, 'Then who can be saved?' " This teaching of Jesus confused even the apostles. Their heritage had taught them that riches were a blessing from God because of one's righteousness. The richer a person was, the more favorable he was to God. If this rich guy wasn't saved, went the logic, what possible hope was there for the poor?

Not only does this doctrine give some mighty greedy people too much assurance but it also discourages many struggling Christians. In addition to the burden of bad health, a financial setback, or a marital problem, here comes a teaching that implies your problem is a sign God is displeased with you! This heartless, ungodly teaching has snuffed out the last flickering flame of many Christians.

Finally, the people who promote this concept bring shame on the church. They turn off clear-thinking people in the unsaved world. It doesn't take a genius to see this for the sham it is. This hollow doctrine has led many people to reject Christ altogether. What long-term appeal is there to a God who is nothing more than the host of the "Greed to Glory" game show?

What the Bible Really Teaches

Agreed, there are some broad teachings in Scripture (and the natural world) that tell us we will have a better quality of life if we play by the rules. For instance, a person who lives a Christlike life is less likely to die from lung cancer than the person who has smoked for forty years, ignoring God's teaching to protect his body (1 Corinthians 6:18, 19). No one can dispute that God promises to bless those who put Him first. The following two passages both allude to this truth:

> Give, and it will be given to you; good measure, pressed down, shaken together, running over, they will pour into your lap. For whatever measure you deal out to others, it will be dealt to you in return.
>
> Luke 6:38 NAS

> But seek first His kingdom and His righteousness; and all these things shall be added to you.
>
> Matthew 6:33 NAS

However, two important points are often missed. First, God isn't guaranteeing us a Las Vegas-style jackpot. He isn't promising to pay back one hundred dollars for every ten we put into the collection plate. God is not a cosmic slot machine that can be "played." God is God. He is sovereign. He is holy. With some very caustic words, Isaiah spoke God's sentiment on this matter to the nation of Israel:

> You turn things around! Shall the potter be considered as equal with the clay, That what is made should say to its maker, "He did not make me"; Or what is formed say to him who formed it, "He has no understanding"?
>
> Isaiah 29:16 NAS

God is in charge, not us. We are here to serve Him, not the other way around. God owes us nothing. Yet He loved us enough to buy us back, clean us up, and give us worth! Because of what He did for us, our future is secure. How dare we try to bribe and coerce our loving Father! As Jesus points out in Luke 17:5–10, even after we have done all we can do, we will still be unworthy servants.

Second, I am unaware of any Scripture where God promises us a lavish life-style. It's just not in there. As a matter of fact, this concept of rich Christianity is a fairly recent one. History is replete with stories of Christians who lost everything they had for Jesus. Jesus even tells us if we aren't willing to put it all on the line for Him, we are unworthy to wear His Name. But here in twentieth-century America, some of us are convinced that being a good Christian is synonymous with having a big house, expensive clothes, and a fat bank account. Only in such a culture could such a heresy flourish!

Whether we like it or not, God didn't put us here just to be happy. He put us here to be holy. "Selective Witnessing" is a prose poem that speaks to this misunderstanding:

It was a week ago last Tuesday that I gave You my heart, Lord. Coming up out of the waters, I knew things were going to be different between You and me. We're going to be best friends, closer than close.

I'm especially excited to have You in my home. I want You to see where I live. It's not perfect, but it's me. This is where I keep all my treasures. All my personal belongings are stored here. By the way, Jesus, You don't mind staying in the guest room, do You? It'll just be for a little while—a few weeks at most. I need to tidy things up just a bit. It's not that I don't want You in the other rooms of my heart. It's just that . . . well, You might not be very comfortable at present. I need to slip a few things into the drawers and under the beds.

What's that, Lord? Why don't I let You help me get rid of them permanently instead? Well, maybe later, but not quite yet. I've lived in some of those rooms for a long time now, Lord. It's hard to say good-bye to all the old nooks and crannies.

Now come on, Lord, don't say that! It's not as if I've put my hand to the plow and I'm looking back. I mean to follow You and You only. You're all that matters. But these days a Christian has to relate. You have to fit in—or no one will listen. How can I let my light shine if everyone thinks I'm crazy?

Compromise? No, I wouldn't call it that. I would refer to it as "selective witnessing." Yeah, that's it, "selective witnessing." I don't want to be too obvious. After all, what good am I if I don't fit in? And Lord, this self-denial stuff just isn't my bag. Nobody lives that way today!

What did You say? . . . It's either Your way or no way. But Lord, I want to be Your disciple! Living for You is all that matters, but I have my rights, too! If I start really taking this discipleship idea seriously, my friends will think I'm a few bricks short of a load!

Living for You is what I want to do, but let's keep it in balance. I don't want to be a fanatic. I want to fit in with my pals. You understand, don't You, Lord . . . Lord?

What God does promise His followers is that He will take care of their *needs*—not necessarily their *whims*. God cares for each of us as He alone knows best. Granted, for some that might mean financial blessings. Others may be blessed with good health, a happy family, an abundance of friends, or a special talent. But we must remember that God's concept of what we need and our concept of what we need may be different.

This point is made very effectively in 2 Corinthians 12:7–10 NAS:

> And because of the surpassing greatness of the revelations, for this reason, to keep me from exalting myself, there was given to me a thorn in the flesh, a messenger of Satan to buffet me—to keep me from exalting myself! Concerning this I entreated the Lord three times that it might depart from me. And He has said to me, "My grace is sufficient for you, for power is perfected in weakness." Most gladly, therefore, I will rather boast about my weaknesses, that the power of Christ may dwell in me. Therefore I am well content with weaknesses, with insults, with distresses, with persecutions, with difficulties, for Christ's sake; for when I am weak, then I am strong.

The Apostle Paul had a "thorn in the flesh." There has been a lot of speculation about this. Maybe his eyesight was failing. Maybe he had epilepsy, or another ailment. Whatever it was, Paul obviously wanted a physical healing. But God denied the request. He knew Paul would exalt himself if he were cured. To keep Paul from falling into this trap, God refused to heal him. But through it all, God never left Paul alone. God's grace was always a fact of life for Paul.

Our Heavenly Father works much like an earthly parent. He wants His kids to have all they can handle. But just like an earthly parent, God often has to say no to foolish requests. Too often, we ask for things that we really don't need or things that might get us into trouble. Earlier in the book, I told you about my failed singing career. Those were discouraging days. No matter how hard I tried, my performances and recording work never really caught on. At that time, I was hurt and angry that all my efforts ended in failure. Today, things are clearer. I understand why God didn't give me enough talent to be a singing success. If He had, I probably would have compromised my convictions and sold out on my faith. That's not easy for me to admit, but it's the truth. God knew I couldn't handle the pressures of the entertainment business, so He spared me a lot of heartache. Today, I am glad He cared enough to deal with me as He did. Just as Paul learned, I, too, am learning that God's grace truly is sufficient.

*"THIS ABOVE ALL:
TO THINE OWN SELF BE
TRUE, AND IT MUST
FOLLOW, AS THE NIGHT
THE DAY, THOU CANST
NOT THEN BE FALSE
TO ANY MAN."*
—WILLIAM SHAKESPEARE

4

Bill, The Word Is Integrity

It began on June 25, 1950, when Communist-controlled North Korean soldiers invaded South Korea. They called it a police action, but for the 580,000 allied troops who died in the conflict, it was a war. During those three years, families all over America were uprooted. Draft notices claimed fathers and sons to a different world. Lives and dreams were put on hold, sometimes never to be realized.

On his radio program, Charles Swindoll related the story of Major General Dean, who was one of the tragedies of the Korean War. On a bleak day during his second winter in a North Korean prison camp, it became clear to Major Dean that his death was near. His captors gave him a few minutes to write a last note to his family. One sentence was directed to his only son: "Tell Bill the word is integrity."

What a legacy for a father to leave his child. Any leader who instills the concept of integrity has given one of the greatest gifts there is. Integrity lasts. No matter how bad things get, integrity is a constant. That's because integrity is an absolute. A person either has it or he doesn't have it. There is no in-between. Sands shift. Wind directions change. Integrity is always on the same steady course.

Our real problem is that there aren't enough integrity role models today. Like any other positive trait, integrity requires self-discipline. It often means saying no to a shortcut. Unfortunately, our society is not known for its restraint. There just aren't very many people we can still look up to. People on the congressional ethics committees are working overtime. Wall Street is so infected by insider trading scandals that large brokerage firms are starting to offer brokers paid prison leave. (Not really.) And as we all know, the credibility of broadcast evangelism is at an all-time low.

Everyday Questions of Integrity

Very little surprises me anymore. However, I never cease to be saddened by the dismal shortage of integrity in the marketplace. Following are three examples of integrity deficits friends have shared with me. I haven't selected these because they are particularly sensational or blatant. As a matter of fact, I'm sharing these stories with you because they are so average. They are so seemingly minor that any one of us could be guilty of the same sort of thing. So if anything I say in this chapter steps on your toes, mine will probably be getting bruised, too.

As I share these accounts with you, don't expect any surprise endings or revolutionary insights. I'm simply relating these events to help us focus on the nature of the problem. Sometimes by seeing it in another person's behavior, we can make personal applications less painfully. (Note: Of course, the names and certain details have been altered.)

Illustration 1. Our first story begins with a friend of mine whom I'll call Roger. Roger used to work as a creative director in an advertising firm. He recently told me one of the reasons he left. It had to do with the owner's basic lack of integrity. Roger told me of a client presentation to which he had accompanied his boss. In the presentation, his employer began to tell the potential client of their firm's capabilities. In the course of the conversation, my friend was shocked to see his boss pull out some advertising samples that their firm had not actually produced. He then went on to tell the client that these were examples of *their* advertising.

Since it was not Roger's presentation, he remained quiet until they had left the client's office. Then he landed on his employer with both feet, demanding an explanation for the lies he had told. His boss explained that their firm "could have" produced a job like the sample he showed, so he had no ethical problem in telling the client that it was his work.

Illustration 2. The second illustration comes from an individual whom I'll call Cathy. As an employee of a nonprofit organization, Cathy has learned firsthand how hard it is to raise funds. There is always more to do than there are dollars with which to do it. Motivating the public to give is always a struggle. Cathy's organization is constantly looking for new ways to generate donations. To this end, they hired a firm that specialized in fund-raising to consult with them on the most effective way to collect contributions. That's when the problem occurred.

The consultants developed a plan to get gifts by using a deceptive tactic. It's called the "composite personality" approach. It is based on the fact that people are usually more willing to give a contribution to help another person than they are to give to help an impersonal organization. The consultants developed a composite person who really didn't exist. They gave that person a name and a set of needs. Then, with the identity established, they began to raise money on behalf of that person. I'm sure the consultants would argue that their "creation" epitomized many of those for whom the money was actually raised, and after all, it was a worthy cause. But Cathy and her organization didn't see it that way. Besides, what was Cathy supposed to say when a donor asked her point-blank, "How is that little guy in the ad getting along?" The campaign was dropped.

Illustration 3. Our third illustration was related to me recently by a young man I'll call James. It all began when he approached me about a job. At first, I couldn't understand why he wanted another position. James had established a remarkable track record with a major retailing chain. Still in his twenties, he had developed the marketing and sales force that had made his store one of the top locations in the national store chain. In less than five years, gross sales had increased by more than 500 percent! Profits were great. His subordinates enjoyed working for him. The owners thought he was the greatest thing since the cash register. His salary was exceptional.

So why did he want to leave, I asked. Although there were several reasons, one reason stood out above all the others. James explained that it was because of a fundamental lack of integrity on the part of the owners. He told me of a number of practices that were, at the least, questionable. One of these practices involved pricing. Here's how it worked: When a customer came in and asked for a discount, frequently the owners would reduce the price by the amount of the sales tax. Then when the customer left, they would write up a falsified out-of-state shipping address. By reporting it as an out-of-state sale, they avoided paying the required sales tax. As far as the owners were concerned, it was just good business. After all, no one knew about it, and they ended up getting full price on the merchandise.

But James, who is a dedicated Christian, saw the sin for what it was. He realized the danger he was in. I'll never forget his concluding comment: "Steve, I just don't want to stay there and become the way they are." I hired him.

"Everyone Has His Price"

Somewhere along the way, you have probably heard a cynical individual make the comment, "Everyone can be bought; everybody has his price." Such commentary on the human condition isn't new. Ancient Greek literature tells of Diogenes and the lantern he carried even in the middle of the day in his search for a man of honor.

I don't believe this is true. If it were true, it would mean there is no one with integrity. Admittedly, too many people do "have their price." You can probably recall a time when someone you admired sold out for a price. It hurts, and it makes you less likely to trust other people, but to suggest that no one has integrity ignores the facts.

There always have been (and always will be) those who cannot be bought at any price. These are men and women for whom the truth is absolute. I count as friends a number of people whom I would trust with anything I have. No matter what the cost, they would not betray me. Despite all that has been written about the betrayal of Jesus, the fact remains that eleven of the twelve apostles remained true to Him until their own deaths. It is not unusual to hear a news story about a corporate executive who lost his job because he blew the whistle on corrupt or dangerous company practices.

We have all heard the old joke about America having the best politicians money can buy. My friend Cal Thomas loves to say that the only politicians with convictions are in prison. The fact is, we live in one of the most squeaky-clean nations on the globe. Our leaders are held to one of the highest levels of accountability anywhere. Certainly there is room for improvement, but there are still a number of honest men and women representing our interests in Washington.

Many people in the business world are concerned about integrity. They really want to deliver their products and services in an ethical, honest manner. I serve on the board of a business advisory council of a Christian university. Recently, we received the results of a survey made of our members. It had asked them to list the topics they would most like to hear discussed in a seminar. At the top of the list was the topic of ethics.

A Friend Who Paid the Price

I have a friend who paid a high price for his integrity: his business. His company manufactured a highly specialized type of equipment that is used in the production of motion pictures. Over several years he had invested heavily in the production of a new and highly sophisticated piece of equipment he hoped to sell worldwide. One of the most important sales was to a major movie studio in Hollywood. Everything was progressing just fine until one fateful day when the news reported that this film firm was about to release a movie that had been widely criticized by Christians.

The news of this project greatly concerned my friend, who is a devout Christian. The more he thought and prayed about the matter, the more convinced he became that he simply could not do business with this studio. Finally, the corporate decision was made not to sell the equipment to the studio. Word of this spread throughout the industry. Soon other studios, misunderstanding my friend's purpose for not selling the equipment to the offending production firm, decided not to order from him.

With the research and development costs my friend's firm had incurred, this slump in sales became devastating. Cash flow dried up. Soon it was obvious—my friend had to either placate his former customers or suffer the consequences.

Through the entire ordeal, he remained true to his beliefs. Sure enough, the company was devastated. But that's not the end of the story. God cares for His own. After my friend had proven where his allegiance really was, God stepped in with the perfect solution. The company was bought by an individual who was close to my friend. He gave my friend a job that was to his liking. Today, with less stress and more time to do what he enjoys most, my friend has never been happier!

I have talked with a number of businesspeople who struggle over the issue of what is right and wrong. While they may not be in the majority, these are people who will not accept a profit if it means taking advantage of someone else. I work with two such businessmen. Clay Young and Jerry Atnip have worked with our company for over a dozen years. In that period of time, we have produced a lot of work for a lot of clients. I can truthfully say I've never seen either one of them knowingly take advantage of a single client.

There have been times when we weren't sure what to do in a given situation. We have often met to discuss certain circumstances and plan the best strategies. Frequently, before making a major presentation, we meet for prayer. One of the things we typically ask from God is that He will help us make an honest and ethical presentation. Despite all of the mistakes we make, there is a godly peace that comes when we seek His counsel first. Somehow, the profits are more fun to spend.

A Personal Survey

The real question is, by its nature, a personal one. Just how honest are you? Even more to the point, how honest am I? Do we have our price? Could any amount of money get us to cheat on our taxes? Could we be tempted to pad a client's time charges? Even more basically, what do we do when a clerk gives us back too much change? Whether we like it or not, these are all questions of integrity.

Obviously, different Christians will see minor points differently. I'll admit there are shades here. There will be slightly varying opinions even among serious-minded Christians. For instance, one person might feel comfortable claiming a marginal tax deduction that another person might not claim. One firm might have no problem trying to win an account away from a competitor, while another firm may feel this sort of aggressiveness is excessive.

The root issue of integrity is a black-and-white one. As we said earlier, integrity is an absolute. You either have it or you don't. Basically, people take two approaches to developing their ethical response.

Some people respond to situations as they come up. They feel that each situation has its own merits and should be reviewed accordingly. This all sounds fine on the surface, but there's a problem: No one does his best thinking in the heat of battle. When the pressure is on, pragmatism can easily replace piety. There will be those inevitable emotional considerations. "I know it's not totally honest, but payroll is due on Friday and we need the money." "Maybe I got that information unethically, but if I don't use it we'll lose the account." "I know I gave them my word, but now things have changed."

To develop a sense of integrity that won't fail us when the heat is turned up, we must take a different approach. We need to develop our basic morality *before* situations arise that will test it. Only in this way can we perform at the level we really desire to perform at. When David went to fight Goliath, he wasn't still looking for stones to put in his sling. He had already done that. When he got before the giant, he was there to "close the deal."

It all boils down to having already asked and answered the basic questions. It means knowing your heart and having sought the heart of God. That way, when you are in a challenging situation, you aren't developing theory—you are applying it.

Three Checkpoints

While it isn't original with me, there is a three-point checklist that can be applied to any situation to help us determine what to do. Frankly, this checklist is difficult to live up to. I struggle with these points on a daily basis. As much as it hurts, I have to admit I have fallen woefully short of these goals many times. By applying these three questions *before* we make a decision, we can avoid a lot of heartache. Most important, we will have the comfort of knowing God is pleased with our actions.

Is what I'm about to do lawful? Will my actions break any civil, criminal, or tax law? Will this behavior be consistent with company regulations and policies? Will it be in conflict with professional standards?

Is what I'm proposing going to be good for everyone involved? Am I helping to build a win-win situation that will allow everyone to gain in the end?

Am I treating the other person the way I would want to be treated? Jesus said, "Therefore whatever you want others to do for you, do so for them, for this is the Law and the Prophets" (Matthew 7:12 NAS).

Such a simple concept, but such a challenge to obey. However, if you show others the same consideration and fairness you would want if the tables were turned (and they might well be one day), all of your relationships will improve. If you run a business, there will be less employee turnover. If you sell products, your customers will refer you to their friends. If you lead at church, others will listen to your counsel because they know you can be trusted. Your concern for others will be evidence of the Spirit's fruit in your life, and only with this Spirit fruit, "love, joy, peace, patience, kindness, goodness, faithfulness, gentleness, self-control" (Galatians 5:22, 23 NAS), can godly success be yours.

Keeping Our Focus

Earlier in this chapter, I told you about three cases where integrity took a backseat. I believe there was a common root problem in each of those cases. That root problem had to do with focus. Often we compromise our integrity the moment we lose our focus. When we forget the big picture and start looking for immediate gratification, we've set ourselves up for a fall. At such times we are likely to panic and do things we might otherwise not do. When we allow ourselves to become too concerned about the here and now (meeting a payroll, signing the contract, and so on), it is very easy to forget the bedrock principles we want to live up to. In other words, it is the struggle between living for the "beautiful by-and-by" and dealing with the "nasty now-and-now."

But Jesus understands all this. He knows we lie to those who should be able to trust us. He knows we cheat and steal in moments of weakness. He knows we are all fallen creatures. That's why He came—because we simply could not do it right without Him! As believers, we have His hand to hold on to. We have His resources to tap. Most of all, we have His blood to forgive our sins. Maybe this is part of the reason Jesus encouraged us to trust Him and not become worried:

> For this reason I say to you, do not be anxious for your life, as to what you shall eat, or what you shall drink; nor for your body, as to what you shall put on. Is not life more than food, and the body than clothing? Look at the birds of the air, that they do not sow, neither do they reap, nor gather into barns, and yet your heavenly Father feeds them. Are you not worth much more than they? And which of you by being anxious can add a single cubit to his life's span? And why are you anxious about clothing? Observe how the lilies of the field grow; they do not toil nor do they spin, yet I say to you that even Solomon in all his glory did not clothe himself like one of these. But if God so arrays the grass of the field, which is alive today and tomorrow is thrown into the furnace, will He not much more do so for you, O men of little faith? Do not be anxious then, saying, "What shall we eat?" or "What shall we drink?" or "With what shall we clothe ourselves?" For all these things the Gentiles eagerly seek; for your heavenly Father knows that you need all these things. But seek first His kingdom and His righteousness; and all these things shall be added to you. Therefore do not be anxious for tomorrow; for tomorrow will care for itself. Each day has enough trouble of its own.
>
> Matthew 6:25–34 NAS

Earlier, I told you there would be parts of this chapter that would step on our toes. Well, I don't know about you, but my toes have just been mowed off at the ankles! Every time I read this passage from Christ's Sermon on the Mount, I am overwhelmed by my own failures. I am so untrusting. My faith is so weak. Yet, as I survey all the miles I've traveled, I can truthfully tell you that God has never failed me. Not even once. There has never been one day when He did not provide all I needed. He has poured me full of His sweet blessings.

With it all, I frequently still try to seize control from God when the going gets rough. When problems arise, I instinctively try to solve them on my own, and sometimes it's not until after I'm in trouble that I call on God for help. Yet I can tell you that on those occasions when I have really trusted God, waited for His solution, and applied His principles, I have never been ashamed of my behavior.

Maybe you can relate to a college professor of mine who also preached for a local church. One day Dr. Carroll Ellis surprised us with this comment: "Sometimes people ask me if I practice what I preach. I always tell them, 'Nooo-ooo, I don't practice what I preach.'" When he was sure he had our attention, he went on, "I preach perfection—and so far I haven't attained it."

Dr. Ellis' comment speaks to my heart on this subject. If what I've said has covered you with a burden of guilt, I'm sorry. That wasn't my purpose. We all make mistakes. The good news is that God forgives us when we fall down, but He does want us to repent of our sins, learn from them, and go on.

If you've lived very long or done very much, you've committed a lot of sins and failed a lot of times. If you are like me, some of those old memories cause you to blush. Even more embarrassing for me is the fact that some of those "old memories" have been made recently. Rarely does a day pass when I don't "drop the ball" spiritually. Maybe you, too, can relate to this frustration. All mortals are frail. We live in a fallen, sinful environment. We all have skeletons in our closets—past mistakes that the Enemy loves to dredge up to make us feel ashamed and useless. But glory be to God, those of us who have received the gift of Jesus' forgiveness can get past the failures and live above our flaws!

Paul had done more damage before he was saved than most of us will ever get around to doing. He had jailed and persecuted Christians all around the Mediterranean. In short, he had done everything he could dream up to hurt the church, yet he was so certain of his forgiveness that he was able to write this to the Christians at Philippi: ". . . but one thing I do: forgetting what lies behind and reaching forward to what lies ahead, I press on toward the goal for the prize of the upward call of God in Christ Jesus" (Philippians 3:13, 14 NAS).

It is probable that some of the Christians Paul had persecuted were in that very Philippian church! How could Paul tell those people he had put his past behind him? How could he bring himself to write to them with the authority of an apostle? Maybe it was because Paul understood the forgiveness of Jesus better than we do. Paul accepted the fact of his forgiveness. He understood that Christianity is a life of looking forward.

What About Restitution?

I wouldn't suggest that there aren't cases where restitution is appropriate. Obviously, if I steal a television set and later repent of that sin, I should return the set to its rightful owner.

Restitution is a matter for personal soul-searching. If you are concerned about something in the past that might require restitution, the following steps may be helpful. First, bring it before God. Submit yourself to His will and seek His direction. Remember, you are His child. He loves you and wants only what is best for you. If you don't sense a clear direction from God, seek out a devout Christian to talk with. Describe the situation as honestly as you can to that person. Listen carefully to his or her suggestions, which might be more objective than your own. If what that person encourages you to do rings true, take the advice.

I hesitate to talk too much about this because some people with tender consciences will worry needlessly. If you are one of these people, please don't grieve too much about the past. After you have made a mistake, it is usually best to pray for forgiveness and go on. As they say, you can't put toothpaste back in the tube. Don't let the devil steal your peace. The word translated "Satan" in Zechariah 3:1 is the same Hebrew word used for "accuser." This gives us some insight into Satan's nature. He knows that one of his best weapons against a Christian with a tender conscience is an unending volley of accusations. The devil delights in reminding us that we are evil, worthless sinners. He enjoys reminiscing with us over past sins. He loves to see us worry about and even doubt our salvation. If your heart is soft, don't allow the devil to do this to you.

There are others who need to repent and may need to make restitution. Unfortunately, these people are often too hardened to realize it. These are the people who have become comfortable with an unethical life-style. They have found an excuse for anything they want to do. I encourage these people to pray for discernment and conviction.

 *Key #4*

The dictionary isn't the only place where integrity comes before success. It's that way in life, too. By determining to be women and men of integrity *before* the time of temptation, we will be better equipped when in the heat of spiritual battle. If we *preact* (plan and pray before the moment of crisis), we will not be forced to *react* in a way we will regret later.

As Dr. Harold Hazelip, a university president and minister, has pointed out:

> Integrity involves more than just having the right set of values; it includes having the strength of will to live with those values. Sometimes our problem is in knowing what to do in a given situation. More often our struggle is in doing what we know we should do. It is not simply a question of knowledge; it is equally a question of courage and determination.

"*FOR I KNOW WHOM I
HAVE BELIEVED, AND AM
PERSUADED THAT HE IS
ABLE TO KEEP THAT WHICH
I HAVE COMMITTED UNTO
HIM AGAINST THAT DAY.*"
—*TIMOTHY* 1:12 *KJV*

5

SELF-CONFIDENCE: A CHRISTIAN PERSPECTIVE

I love New York City. There is something about that town that gets this Nashville boy's blood perking. Everywhere you go there is beautiful art, fantastic architecture, limitless shopping, and fabulous restaurants. The city throbs with every imaginable appeal: Broadway, Times Square, Little Italy, Wall Street, Carnegie Hall, and Rockefeller Center. Whether it is business or pleasure, all I need is an excuse and a plane ticket.

Recently, my wife, Bonnie, and I took a short trip to the Big Apple to enjoy the sights. In addition to all the regular attractions, we saw an unexpected one that taught us a real lesson.

It was Friday night and we had just finished a wonderful dinner in Chinatown. Being the "big spender" I am, I said, "Come on, let's take the subway back up to midtown." With that, we went down the stairs and got on the train. Now, for the rest of this story to make sense, you have to bear in mind that in Nashville we don't have subways, and it's a strain on my cerebral limits to correctly navigate the New York subway system. Despite the way my wife might tell this, I *did* in fact get us on the right train—sort of. It was the right train, but it was going in the wrong direction. Instead of going uptown on the R Train, we were on the R Train headed for Brooklyn. Thirty minutes later, there we sat (in our best clothes) waiting for the return train in a Brooklyn subway station late on Friday night. As we waited, we witnessed a very diverse parade of humanity. But the biggest surprise was yet to come.

Suddenly, some of the people began to mumble. They were talking about someone coming into the station. I knew that anyone who could capture the attention of this crowd had to be worth seeing. I overheard one of the locals whisper, "He's a punker." At that moment, he stepped around the corner. Sure enough, it was one of those "punkers" I'd heard about. His head was shaved almost clean except for a five-inch-high, orange Mohawk. He wore an earring that went through his ear in three places. Even his nose was pierced. His black leather jacket was weighted down with metal studs, and his boots had metal spikes protruding. His appearance was ominous, so we instinctively gave him plenty of space.

The train arrived, and immediately all but two of the seats were taken—the one on the right and the one on the left of our punker friend. Not even the folks in Brooklyn would sit with him! Well, I wasn't about to stand with seats available, so we walked over and asked if he would slide over so we could sit beside him. He did. There we sat, Bonnie to my left and Mr. Mohawk to my right. I guess we deserved the stares we got. Apparently, Brooklyn wasn't in the habit of seeing suits and studded leather jackets together on the subway. Everyone seemed anxious to see if this angry-looking young man would produce a knife to slice and dice the guy from Nashville.

As we traveled, we talked. Frankly, I liked this unusual fellow. Finally, I asked if he lived in Brooklyn. "No," he responded, "I come from Nashville, Tennessee!"

Truth in the Old Adage

Every time I recall that night on a New York subway, I'm reminded of the old adage, "Things are frequently not as they appear."

We've all heard stories of gold prospectors who thought they had struck the mother lode, only to find that all they had was a worthless haul of pyrite, or "fool's gold." Every once in a while we read a news story about a merchant who, thinking it was the real thing, accepted counterfeit money in exchange for his property.

So it is with the concept of self-confidence. Everywhere we turn there are books, TV shows, and cassette tapes promising to give us self-confidence. As with so many other things, the promise frequently exceeds reality. We all want to be assured and self-confident but so few of us ever achieve a true, lasting form of it. Instead, we buy into a worldly system that counterfeits the real article. Without a spiritual foundation, self-confidence becomes nothing more than another weapon from the arsenal of Satan.

The Big Lie

The prospector and the merchant both made the same mistake: They based their behavior on faulty assumptions. They believed a lie.

In the same way, many of us have bought into a lie. We spend a lifetime trying to overcome our feelings of inadequacy in all the wrong ways, and all the time, the devil is rooting us on.

There are a lot of people who are convinced they are no good to anyone. The world really has no place for them. These people are sure that everyone (and I do mean *everyone*) is better than they are. When these people look in the mirror, all they see is a failure. They are never comfortable in a crowd. As far as they are concerned, no one ever looks at them with anything other than a critical eye. These individuals have absolutely no self-confidence, and what's more, they see no good reason to feel different about themselves. Their lives have been filled with one defeat after another.

Folks like these can relate to the lady who went to the psychiatrist to get help with her inferiority complex. Finally, after several counseling sessions, the psychiatrist leaned back in his chair and said, "Lady, the good news is that you don't have a complex. The bad news is that you really *are* inferior!"

A Very Personal Pain

The problem? Most of us really don't get a lot of encouragement from our family and friends. Too often, the people we associate with are, either consciously or unconsciously, very detrimental to our self-esteem and confidence.

The concept of self-confidence is an intangible and delicate one. Too often, it is a fleeting thing. Any athlete will tell you that self-confidence is essential to win. Frequently, two very comparable teams will end a game with a wide spread on the scoreboard. Everything appeared equal. All the players on both teams were healthy. Both coaches had great game plans. Why, then, did one team beat the other so badly? I believe the determining factor was each team's self-confidence level. If one team captures the momentum early, the other team's confidence level is likely to drop. Unless something is done quickly, the losing team begins a fatal hemorrhage of self-confidence.

When We Were Kids

This happens on an individual basis, too. We can all remember the kids in school who were the losers. No matter what they did, no one liked them. They were always being laughed at. They could do the same thing Patty Popular or Cary Cool did, but instead of being accepted they got ridiculed.

In 1974, Janis Ian wrote and recorded one of the most penetrating songs I've ever heard. I suspect the reason for its popularity may have rested in the fact that it hit a hot button for so many people. Probably more people than would want to admit it were able to relate to the message in this song. The title is, "At Seventeen." Here are some of the lyrics:

> I learned the truth at seventeen
> That love was meant for beauty queens
> and high school girls with clear-skinned smiles
> who married young, and then retired.
> The Valentines I never knew
> The Friday night charades of youth
> were spent on one more beautiful
> At seventeen, I learned the truth
> And those of us with ravaged faces
> lacking in the social graces . . .

. . . and those whose names were never called
when choosing sides for basketball.
It was long ago, and far away
The world was younger than today
and dreams were all they gave for free
to ugly duckling girls like me.

A Personal Story

Can you relate to that song? I can. I know exactly how she felt. That song could have been written about me. For whatever reason, I got off to a bad start early in my school years. One rejection followed another. Before long, I believed what the other kids said about me. My self-confidence evaporated. I accepted the role they wrote for me. I became one of those "ugly duckling" kids no one had any use for. My childhood years were rough ones. I learned early what it was like to lie in bed at night dreading the next day at school. I know how it feels to leave a loving home in the morning and enter hostile territory at the schoolhouse door.

Grade school was filled with one denial after another. I was the brunt of many jokes. When another child accidentally touched me, he would rush to touch someone else and say, "Steve Diggs contamination, no gives!" I was usually about the last boy to be picked for any ball team. Getting beaten up after school was something I excelled at.

High school was just more of the same. I knew how it felt to sit at home while the other kids were running around together. I knew the feeling of hoping for an invitation that never arrived. I was convinced no girl in her right mind would ever go out with me.

The more I was rejected, the more I doubted my own worth,

and the more I doubted my own worth, the more I got rejected. It was a vicious cycle, one I felt incapable of breaking. It wasn't until my senior year that the cycle was finally broken, and the way it happened was sheer accident.

I didn't have anything to lose, so I decided to go after my dream of becoming an entertainer. During my senior year, I began singing on local TV shows. Gradually, schoolmates began to notice. In the spring, the school announced there would be tryouts to select two student speakers for the graduation ceremony. Again, I didn't have anything to lose. I prepared the best speech I could write, practiced it tirelessly, and went to the audition. God must have known what a critical point I was at. I'll always praise Him for the way He blessed that audition. I was selected to speak to my class on graduation night!

Things began to change immediately. I took one of the prettiest girls in the area as my date that night. The speech was a success. There was a newspaper write-up about it. Congratulatory letters and statements came from everywhere. For the first time in my life, I realized I could do it!

A few days later, I began a week of sales training to prepare me to sell books that summer. Sales school taught me to use the abilities God had given me. It taught me the importance of a good attitude. I finally understood that I wasn't a born loser. I learned that self-confidence was a state of mind—a perception. For the first time, I realized I had allowed other kids to intimidate me all my life. I realized they had all the same fears and self-doubt I had. The only difference was, I hadn't seen through their facades. They had actually convinced me that I was inferior to them. I had bought into all the negativism others had laid on me! I'd simply played out the role they had assigned to me. I had become the victim of a self-fulfilling prophecy. What a revelation!

By the end of the summer, I had established a successful sales record. That fall, I started college in another city. It was a chance to start over, a fresh beginning. I could be whatever I chose to be. I chose to be self-confident. I chose to be a winner. Things were very different. I wasn't the same kid who had gone to sleep dreading the next day at school.

A new cycle was formed. One success led to another. The confidence I had in myself led others to believe in me, too. I soon realized that other people like to be around a person who has a good self-image. I became involved in a number of campus activities and things I had never dared to do before. Soon I had a daily radio show on a local station. I even worked for the college, traveling and speaking on behalf of the school. There were articles about my recording work in the newspapers.

The trend that had developed for the first seventeen years of my life was abolished, and a completely new trend was established.

But the Trouble Was . . .

I wish the above story ended with, "And he lived happily ever after." But that's not the case. Something strange happened. Instead of developing a constructive, productive self-image, I went to an unhealthy extreme. It was as if I had pulled out of the ditch on one side of the road only to land squarely in the ditch on the other side!

My newfound self-confidence mutated into arrogance and pride. It wasn't long before my friends began to wonder why I had changed. As I became more conceited, I lost more friends, and as sin always does, my problem with pride brought sadness.

Maybe this is why God warns us to constantly be on the

lookout for pride. In Proverbs 6:16–19, where God lists seven things He hates, number one on the list is "haughty eyes." From Genesis through Revelation, the Scriptures warn us over and over about the cancerous effect pride has on the human heart. You might want to get a concordance and make a study of pride in the Bible. For now, let's note just a few of the instances:

> Pride goes before destruction, And a haughty spirit before stumbling. It is better to be of a humble spirit with the lowly, Than to divide the spoil with the proud.
>
> Proverbs 16:18, 19 NAS

> "Behold, I am against you, O arrogant one," Declares the Lord God of hosts, "For your day has come, The time when I shall punish you."
>
> Jeremiah 50:31 NAS

> Behold, this was the guilt of your sister Sodom: she and her daughters had pride. . . .
>
> Ezekiel 16:49 RSV

> For from within, out of the heart of men, proceed the evil thoughts and fornications, thefts, murders, adulteries, deeds of coveting and wickedness, as well as deceit, sensuality, envy, slander, pride and foolishness. All these evil things proceed from within and defile the man.
>
> Mark 7:21–23 NAS

> For all that is in the world, the lust of the flesh and the lust of the eyes and the boastful pride of life, is not from the Father, but is from the world.
>
> 1 John 2:16 NAS

A Godly Balance

I was like a TV set with the vertical hold out of order. The extremely low self-image I had grown up with had been replaced by an equally damaging conceit. Thankfully, God brought me to my senses. He helped me reset the vertical hold of my life. Through prayer, study, and meditation, He brought the harmonious balance that was missing.

Now don't misunderstand. It is still a daily struggle to keep this balance. Just as Paul admitted he had a conflict between the spiritual and the fleshly natures (Romans 7:14–25), I fight a battle for balance every day. Although this balanced approach may be difficult to maintain, it is joyfully simple to understand.

Actually it is all wrapped up in the realization that pride is often based on an ungodly form of competition with others. You see, pride occurs when I attempt to gain my worth by comparing myself with other people. The fruit of such comparisons will always be rotten. This type of comparative pride building is always damaging in at least one of two ways.

First, if I compare myself with someone who is inferior to me in some way, the result will be conceit, pride, and vainglory. Such was the problem Jesus was dealing with when He presented this parable to a group of self-righteous individuals who based their false pride on unfavorable comparisons with others:

Two men went up into the temple to pray, one a Pharisee, and the other a tax-gatherer. The Pharisee stood and was praying thus to himself, "God, I thank Thee that I am not like other people: swindlers, unjust, adulterers, or even like this tax-gatherer. I fast twice a week; I pay tithes of all that I get." But the tax-gatherer, standing some distance away, was even unwilling to lift up his eyes to heaven, but was beating his breast, saying, "God, be merciful to me, the sinner!" I tell you, this man went down to his house justified rather than the other; for every one who exalts himself shall be humbled, but he who humbles himself shall be exalted.

Luke 18:10–14 NAS

Jesus makes it clear that the Pharisee's condescending attitude is not acceptable in the Christian ethic. Notice to whom Jesus says the Pharisee was praying: himself, not God. What a subtle way our Saviour has of making a point! There's room for only one God in any person's life. When we trust in ourselves, we usurp God's proper role in our lives.

More important, look at how the tax-gatherer introduces himself to the Father. He refers to himself not as "a sinner" but as "*the* sinner." What was God's response to such humility? Two beautiful gifts: forgiveness and exaltation.

On the other hand, if we compare ourselves with others who are superior to us, we will feel worthless, ashamed, and inhibited. In this scenario, we can develop a self-image that is different but just as harmful as pride. Here we run the risk of minimizing the gifts God has given us.

Most people who mistake this false form of humility for the true humility God wants us to have experience untold sadness and misery. By constantly comparing their failures with others' successes, they develop unhealthy self-images. Remember, if you lose confidence in yourself, it will probably make the vote unanimous.

With this as our framework, it becomes clear that it is inappropriate for anyone to either exalt or destroy himself (Ephesians 2:8, 9). As Christians, we are neither to look up nor down to anyone. Romans 2:11 tells us God has no "pets": "For there is no partiality with God." We are all equal. Paul speaks further of this balanced approach in Romans 12:3 NAS:

> For through the grace given to me I say to every man among you not to think more highly of himself than he ought to think; but to think so as to have sound judgment, as God has allotted to each a measure of faith.

God's Plan for You

I believe that the balanced approach God wants for us is found in Galatians 6:4 NAS: "But let each one examine his own work, and then he will have reason for boasting in regard to himself alone, and not in regard to another."

The key to a healthy self-image is to do your own personal best. It means using the gifts God has given you to their fullest. If you sell for a living, deliver the best products and services there are. If you are a physician, care for every patient as though he or she were the President of the United States. If you teach, make it your daily prayer to touch young hearts in unforgettable ways. If you are an employee, serve your company as if it were your own.

Finally, keep all of your comparisons intensely personal. Compare your performance today only with your performance yesterday. Never compare yourself (favorably or unfavorably) with others.

Defining Our Terms

Frankly, I have become a little uncomfortable with the term *self-confidence*. This term means different things to different people. I'm afraid that in many cases the connotation is not even Christian. Far too often, people in our society use this term in reference to some capacity they have within themselves. We live in a humanistic, fallen world. We are being told that this is the New Age of enlightenment. We are all gods. We have the power to frame, chart, and control our own destinies. The power of life and death lies within us. We have the ability to forgive our own sins. We can find truth by looking within ourselves. We are the creations of our own thoughts.

As a Christian, I must reject this philosophy. My source of strength and my worth do not come from within me. Every aspect of my being—physical, spiritual, and intellectual—come from God. Without God, I understand that there is nothing.

Before we go any further, let's take a little test. Suppose you were asked to rate your self-confidence level on a scale of 1 to 10. If 10 were an absolutely perfect self-image, where would you be? Would you be a 10? A 6? A 1? Maybe a 0? Maybe you would rank yourself at below 0.

How would you describe yourself to someone you've never met? What statement would you make to announce your status or self-worth? Would you talk about your job? Your hobbies? The power you wield? One of your abilities? Your physical appearance?

A Scriptural Approach

For me, Romans is one of the most transforming books in the Bible. As I've come to know this book better, my concept of God has changed. Romans has made me love Jesus more. I especially like the way Paul begins this letter. He probably wrote it from Corinth in about A.D. 56. He was writing to a group of Christians whom he had never met.

How would he introduce himself to them? What could he say at the very beginning that would best describe him to these readers? What phrase could he use that would immediately tell them where he was coming from? Let's see how he describes himself in Romans 1:1 NAS: "Paul, a bond-servant of Christ Jesus, called as an apostle, set apart for the gospel of God."

Did you notice what Paul considers most important about himself? Although he enjoys the freedom and prestige that comes with being a Roman citizen by birth, Paul still introduces himself as a servant of Christ. To be even more precise, he said he was a bond-servant of Christ. The Greek word for *bond-servant* actually means "slave." Paul saw himself as one who relinquished his own freedom to serve another Master.

Now, if someone were to ask me to describe myself, I probably wouldn't start by announcing that I'm someone's slave. I would be more inclined to brag about my accomplishments, my family, or my job—anything but being someone else's slave!

Paul understood what I often fail to see. He had come to appreciate his honored position. For him, it was a high compliment to be called a slave of Jesus. But what about all the difficulties, beatings, imprisonments, and ridicule? What about all that?

Our Honored Position in Christ

Ed Bartley, a friend of mine who serves on the Nashville police force, recently shared a story that helped me understand Paul's attitude better. Several years ago, the President of the United States visited Nashville. Ed was asked to serve on the detail in charge of protecting him. The special assignment meant working extra hours. It took Ed away from his family. He ended up catching the flu because of the exposure. So, why did he do it when he could have avoided it? The reason he agreed to serve was that it was such an honor.

When we realize what an honor it is to serve Jesus, we will boast in our slavehood right along with Paul. By knowing who our Master is, our self-image will be strong and balanced. We'll know who we're trying to please. The awareness that our Master will take care of all our needs will give us confidence to stand firm. We won't be weak and timid in times of intimidation. When the boss or a client asks us to compromise, we'll have the self-respect to remain true to our convictions.

Our Source of Confidence

When we realize how much God loves us, what He went through to buy us back from the devil, and what a great forgiveness we have received, it should overwhelm us! When we finally understand how much God cares for us, we can face life boldly with an unstoppable confidence. We are children of the King!

The difference in the way an unsaved individual views self-confidence and the way a Christian understands it has to do with how each person perceives the *source* of self-confidence. A person who doesn't know Jesus has a hollow, shallow, empty form of self-confidence. It begins and ends within himself. Ultimately, there is no real foundation to his self-confidence—no higher Source.

Men in the construction business will tell you that working dozens of stories above the ground brings with it a number of dangers most of us don't know about. Sometimes foremen will warn young workers not to "lean against the wind" when they get up to the job site. These veterans know that the wind will sometimes begin blowing so gently that the worker may unconsciously begin to lean against it. Then when the wind suddenly is no longer there, the worker can fall to his death.

A person who says he or she has self-confidence but doesn't know the Lord is leaning against the wind. Self-confidence with no frame of reference leads only to confusion, self-doubt, and defeat. It is a fraudulent life-style. There is no substance to the form. Everything that person has built on is likely to be gone one day, and on that day he or she will be left entirely alone. There will be no strong hands to catch him.

A Christian, on the other hand, has a right to have confidence because he realizes the Source of his confidence. His slaveship to God has given him worth and purpose. Ultimately, his value does not rest within himself but with and in God. This brings the child of God a level of peace and assurance that the world cannot comprehend or take away.

You've Got to Serve Somebody

Several years ago, Bob Dylan released a record entitled, "You've Got to Serve Somebody." He was exactly right. We all have to serve somebody. That may not be a popular concept today in our self-glorifying society. As Americans, we are taught that we serve no one, but that's not really the truth. The Bible tells us we are all slaves:

Do you not know that when you present yourselves to someone as slaves for obedience, you are slaves of the one whom you obey, either of sin resulting in death, or of obedience resulting in righteousness?

Romans 6:16 NAS

The real question is, whose slave are you? Who calls the shots in your life? Are you ruled by the pressures of the world, your lusts, your ambitions, or by God? By trying to serve the world, you will always be filled with uncertainty. Your decisions will always leave you jittery. There will be no real confidence. But with God, you will have a sense of balance that leads to self-confidence and self-respect.

Learning and accepting God's claim on our lives gives us fulfillment. No doubt you have heard someone say, "I want to *find* myself." I remember the confusion and wanderlust of my earlier years. Once, as a college student, I struck out on my motorcycle to find myself. Several days, four states, and one wreck later, I finally returned home. I still hadn't found me.

Jesus tells us how to find ourselves:

And he who does not take his cross and follow after Me is not worthy of Me. He who has found his life shall lose it, and he who has lost his life for My sake shall find it.

Matthew 10:38, 39 NAS

The Great Adventure

I suspect that the most secure people anywhere are those who have accepted the great adventure of following Christ wherever He leads them. These people have a real sense of mission that is so important it becomes all-encompassing. The person who is wise enough to accept the Great Master's purpose and goal for his or her life is the one who will have true self-confidence. The writer of Proverbs tells us that the outgrowth of godly wisdom is this sort of self-confidence:

> Then you will walk in your way securely, And your foot will not stumble. When you lie down, you will not be afraid; When you lie down, your sleep will be sweet. Do not be afraid of sudden fear, Nor of the onslaught of the wicked when it comes; For the Lord will be your confidence, And will keep your foot from being caught.
>
> Proverbs 3:23–26 NAS

The key to the whole issue is in remembering where our value and worth come from. Paul realized how futile it was to have confidence in the flesh. He understood, as we should, that all goodness, all worth, and all confidence come from God:

> Beware of the dogs, beware of the evil workers, beware of the false circumcision; for we are the true circumcision, who worship in the Spirit of God and glory in Christ Jesus and put no confidence in the flesh, although I myself might have confidence even in the flesh. If anyone else has a mind to put confidence in the flesh, I far more: circumcised the eighth day, of the nation of Israel, of the tribe of Benjamin, a Hebrew of Hebrews; as to the Law, a Pharisee; as to zeal, a persecutor of the church; as to the righteousness which is in the Law, found blameless. But whatever things

were gain to me, those things I have counted as loss for the sake of Christ.

Philippians 3:2–7 NAS

Isn't it interesting how God works? In His scheme, self-confidence is the outgrowth of brokenness. Only when we fall before Him and recognize His right to claim our every talent, ability, and achievement do we gain the confidence to accept life as it comes.

---

*"BLESSED IS THE MAN
WHO HAS A SKIN OF THE
RIGHT THICKNESS.
HE CAN WORK HAPPILY
IN SPITE OF ENEMIES
AND FRIENDS."*

—HENRY T. BAILEY

6

THE IMPORTANCE
OF BEING LIKABLE

A very human trait evidenced itself in our son, Joshua, when he was only four. It happened because of a slight miscommunication between the two of us. Before heading out of town on a business trip, I had that little pep talk fathers and sons have had since the Stone Age. You know the one. It goes something like, "While I'm gone, son, you'll be the man of the house. Take good care of your mother and sisters."

Usually, a simple comment like this can be made with utter safety. The hope is that the little fellow will remember to help out while Dad is gone. Doesn't seem too complicated, does it? But that particular day something very strange happened. To the best I can figure, it must have occurred somewhere in that critical eighteen inches between my mouth and Joshua's ears, because what I thought I said and what Joshua heard were two very different things. Apparently, what he thought he heard was something like, "You are now the supreme boss of this household—the unquestioned dictator."

Not knowing about this miscommunication, I winged off without a care in the world. It wasn't until I phoned home that night that it occurred to me we had a problem. As I recall, Bonnie didn't waste much time on pleasantries. In icy, clipped words, she said, "I am going to put your son on the line. I want you to explain to him that it is not his job to send his sisters and *me* to bed—and announce that he's going to sit up and watch TV."

Unfortunately, vying for power isn't something that ends with childhood. I am writing this chapter from a hotel room in a large southeastern city. I'm here as one of the judges for an Addy Awards contest (where we'll be giving awards for excellence in creative advertising). We have just completed two days of judging. Although we had very diverse opinions on professional matters, we blended together wonderfully. We have come to really like one another. Because we got along so well, the judging was a success.

I can't help but contrast this to a similar event that recently happened in another city. In that awards contest, there was one judge who insisted on dominating the whole affair. He seemed convinced that he had cornered the market on advertising knowledge. Most of the other judges deferred to him and allowed him to determine the winners. This individual seemed satisfied only when he controlled the other judges.

The point is simple: Power should be seen as an awesome gift from God, not something to be usurped from others. Like Joshua, there is something within many of us that doesn't want to pay the rightful price of leadership.

As adults, we need to realize that power isn't something to

be seized or snatched away from others. Instead, power is best enjoyed when one receives it freely from his or her peers, when it is given away. Yet isn't it interesting how so often people choose to seize rather than earn power?

Lest I leave this point unclear, let me explain what I mean by "earning power." Ultimately, power is like any other gift: it is bestowed by a loving, omnipotent God, who allows us to use it for His glory, not our own. So it follows that when God gives power to one of His servants, it is to be wielded with fear and trepidation. Such an attitude will help those who have been given power to remember the responsibility of its stewardship.

The Relationship Between Power, Success, and Being Liked

The success of many a business is greatly dependent upon how well liked the people who run that business are. If that business wants to be more successful, those people who run it must make it a point to be better liked.

A good example of this can be seen in many small towns. If you drive around for a while and look at enough cars, a pattern will soon emerge. This little study will quickly tell you which car dealer in the area is most popular. It is evident by the high percentage of cars with that dealer's logo on the trunk lid. Granted, you could argue that the dealer sells more cars because he is the biggest dealer or because he has more locations, but it goes back to a more fundamental question than that: Why is this dealer the biggest? Why does he have more locations? Why does he sell the most cars? It is at least partially because the people who run that dealership are better liked than their competitors.

A similar study can be made about banks. When you think

about it, almost any bank in a community offers virtually the same products and services the other banks do. Sure, there may be slight differences in the rates charged on loans and earned on deposits, but overall, the offerings are very similar.

Over the years, our advertising firm has been successful in promoting a number of banks. Frequently, these banks were neither the biggest nor the oldest in their communities. Yet we often succeeded by producing advertising that presented the employees more prominently than the products. Many customers select a bank based upon how well they like the people at that bank. Our advertising has often featured bankers engaged in their favorite nonbanking activity or hobby. By taking this "no stuffed shirt" approach, our readers realize that the people at the bank are just plain folks, too. In this age of impersonal machine banking, that is an appealing message. But as we tell the banks, if this sort of advertising is going to work, it has to be truthful. The bank's management has to realize how critical it is for every employee to be a real friend to the customers. The wise bank president understands that his real assets are not in the vault. His real assets all go home at closing time, and if he can help these "assets" become more likable, the bank will become more successful.

To cut to the chase: Decisions are not always made exclusively on the merit of the product, or even the price of that product. Frequently, buying decisions are based on how well liked the people are who promote the product. Mom used to tell us kids, "You can always attract more flies with honey than you can with vinegar." Although I never saw any good reason to attract flies, her point was a solid one: You should build the relationship before you try to persuade someone to deal with you.

It is my understanding that Japanese businesspeople put a high value on developing a personal friendship *before* forging a business relationship. Isn't it sad that the same cannot be said about the way we do business in the West? If Westerners (especially those of us who serve Christ) followed this progression, business litigation and aggravation would hit an all-time low!

In the mid-seventies, when we opened the agency, we gave it an unusual name. Instead of calling it Steve Diggs & Associates or Steve Diggs & Company, we called it Steve Diggs & Friends. We wanted even our name to sound likable. Over the years, it has paid off. We still get comments from people who tell us they appreciate our friendly sounding name.

Two Ways to Gain Influence

Why do so many of us have so much trouble gaining influence? Maybe we are missing the forest and bumping our noses on the trees. The basics of being influential are simple to understand. It's the application that can be tough.

As we have already discussed, you cannot lead other people without some degree of influence over those people. The very essence of leadership involves influence. This influence can be gained in two ways.

First, as our earlier examples showed, you can seize control. You can insist on having your way. You can bully and push. This approach will eventually end in either a loss of respect and influence or a siege mentality where you are forced to fight and coerce those around you. There is very little joy in this type of existence.

The second approach to gaining influence over those you want to lead is best illustrated by Jesus' style of leadership.

He never grabbed people and forced them into service. That just wasn't His style. Instead, Jesus urged would-be followers to count the cost of their decision:

> Whoever does not carry his own cross and come after Me cannot be My disciple. For which one of you, when he wants to build a tower, does not first sit down and calculate the cost, to see if he has enough to complete it? Otherwise, when he has laid a foundation, and is not able to finish, all who observe it begin to ridicule him, saying, "This man began to build and was not able to finish." . . . So therefore, no one of you can be My disciple who does not give up all his own possessions.
>
> Luke 14:27–30, 33 NAS

One reason Jesus Christ has had more followers over the last two thousand years than any other individual in history may well be centered in His personal approach. His followers understand that there is absolutely nothing coercive about His appeal. They know that Jesus wants only the best for them. His followers respond with love and obedience because they understand that His love came first (1 John 4:19). So, for the true follower, Jesus can make no request that is too great to obey. Now, that's real influence!

Just like Jesus, if we want to be successful, we must first have influence over those we want to lead. To gain this influence, we should first earn it. This requires servanthood. If we want to succeed in leadership as Jesus did, we must first be willing to serve as Jesus served. Now, isn't that an interesting concept: Servanthood Leadership. It doesn't fit in very well with this world's approach, does it? So, what does the approach involve?

Let's start with something it *doesn't* involve. Servanthood

Leadership doesn't mean being weak-kneed. Many people have confused leadership with compromise. We frequently see this sort of thing in the political realm where, in an effort to be liked and followed, a person sells out his convictions on key issues. While negotiation has its place, backing down on one's bedrock beliefs is never appropriate.

Although those who are being led may pretend to like leaders who back down, their gut-level feelings are usually quite different. It's tough to admire anyone you can't respect. Generally, followers come to loathe, ridicule, and distrust such a leader.

Four Characteristics of Servanthood Leadership

1. Development of goals that benefit those who follow you. The most likable and successful leaders are those who communicate the "big picture" to their associates. An employee who knows his employer has an "I win, you win" attitude will follow anywhere he's led. He knows his leader *really* cares for him. He has the calm assurance that can come only when he knows his employer looks to the needs of others before his own.

Notice how Jesus' idea of leadership parallels this:

> I am the good shepherd; the good shepherd lays down His life for the sheep. He who is a hireling, and not a shepherd, who is not the owner of the sheep, beholds the wolf coming, and leaves the sheep, and flees, and the wolf snatches them, and scatters them. He flees because he is a hireling, and is not concerned about the sheep. I am the good shepherd; and I know My own, and My own know Me, even as the Father knows Me and I know the Father; and I lay down My life for the sheep.
>
> John 10:11–15 NAS

This is one reason I encourage every employer to offer his employees merit incentives of some sort. When the business has grown, a profit-sharing program is a wise consideration. Even in the earliest stages, a thoughtful employer needs to recognize an excellent associate. This may be as simple as a kind word or a thank-you note with a twenty-dollar bill. In our firm, we occasionally bring in a meal for the creative staff when they are putting in extra effort on a tight deadline. When we have had an especially good month, we sometimes include an unexpected bonus in everyone's paycheck.

Coach Don Myers is a living example of this leadership philosophy. As a basketball coach at a small Southern university, his budgets are always tight. His facilities are somewhat limited. He loses a lot of talent to the bigger schools. With it all, Don turns out a winning team year in and year out. At this writing, the team is 30 and 0 for the season!

This man has succeeded where others would have failed because he puts as much emphasis on attitude as he does on talent. His players know he cares for them personally. He helps them see, dream, and comprehend the "big picture." Every player knows what to expect from every other player. Don frequently overwhelms the opponent by rotating eight or nine players evenly throughout a game. There are no prima donnas on a Don Myers basketball team. Everybody pulls together for the common good because they all have a common goal.

2. Willingness on the leader's part to roll up his own shirtsleeves and get involved. I have always been touched by an example of Servanthood Leadership that Jesus displayed in John 21. Actually, mention of it comes and goes so fast that it could easily be missed in a casual reading. The chapter opens by relating an appearance of Jesus to some disciples after His resurrection.

The men had spent the night getting tossed around in a little boat on the Galilean Sea. Despite their best efforts, the nets kept coming up with zeros. As morning came, Jesus stood on the shore and discussed the fishing business with them. When they admitted to a slow night, Jesus miraculously filled their nets with fish. *Ah, our example of Servanthood Leadership,* you might be thinking. Well, it is *an* example, but it's not *the* example I want us to notice.

We are told that, a few minutes later, when the disciples were on shore, Jesus was busily cooking breakfast for the hungry crew (John 21:9). Wow! What a sight! Here we see the undisputed Ruler of the Universe serving His staff as a short-order cook! What a picture. What an example to those of us who follow Him.

Contrast Jesus' approach to what we generally see in today's business (and even church) world. No one dares to take the boss's parking place. Members in the church wouldn't dream of disagreeing with the minister. The first, biggest, and best of everything is extracted by the chairman. When the manager needs something produced, everyone else's jobs lose priority.

No employee in any organization will work any harder than the owner. If you want your employees to arrive early, work late, and strive for excellence, you will have to do three things: arrive earlier, work later, and strive even harder for excellence. People follow examples much better than they follow orders.

3. High level of Christ-oriented confidence. People want to follow other people who exude real confidence. It gives them a greater sense of security. For Christians, this should come fairly easily. We are followers of Jesus. He has all the answers. Jesus is our Confidence. He has promised to care for our every need, big and little. It should not be hard for us to have a deeply felt confidence, not because of ourselves but because of what Jesus has done for us.

This form of confidence can benefit those we lead in at least two ways. First, as we've already seen, most people derive a sense of well-being when they follow a leader who displays an air of decisiveness and direction.

Second, a leader can be a much better witness for Christ if others see Christ reflected in his or her own behavior patterns. Jesus becomes much more appealing to unsaved individuals when they have a godly leader who doesn't become flustered and worried at every troublesome turn in the road. Such a leader's serenity and peace in the middle of rough seas can serve as a strong witness to those he leads. As in so many other circumstances, a Christian's worldview at such difficult times can be most appealing and inviting.

4. Enthusiasm with an eye toward the eternal. The leader, more than anyone else, must believe in the mission. He must be totally committed to the task. You cannot kindle a fire in another person's heart until it is burning within your own. The least any follower should be able to expect from a leader is an upbeat, optimistic attitude that rarely fails. The president of any corporation ought to be the fastest-walking, biggest-dreaming, most encouraging, and generally the happiest individual in that company. Sure, there will be problems and setbacks, but a Christian leader is familiar with Revelation 21. He knows that these last sentences of the Bible promise an eternal victory. Why waste too much time worrying about the temporal?

It has always intrigued me how so many bright, well-educated people manage to fail while others with less talent and education often succeed. One major study concluded that only 15 percent of successes and promotions were because of technical know-how. The other 85 percent were the result of correct thinking. Our success will be governed far more by our attitude than our aptitude. As motivational speaker and author Zig Ziglar is fond of saying, "We often need a checkup from the neck up."

As you may know, the word *enthusiasm* comes from the two Greek words *en theos*, meaning "God within." With God inside us, there isn't much we can't do. Christians have always had this assurance.

In the year A.D. 62, Paul was in a dark, depressing prison, probably under the streets of Rome. He didn't know what the future held. Ever since he had given his life to Jesus, things had been rough. Now they were terrible. Would he be beaten and freed, or would the executioner walk in and end his life? Such deprivation and uncertainty would have caused many of us to despair, yet Paul's words were bold and confident. He had never lost his faith and enthusiasm for Jesus. In Philippians 4:13 NKJV, he says, "I can do *all* things through Christ who strengthens me" (my italics). What a testimony to godly enthusiasm!

A Final Thought . . .

Before we wrap this up, I want to add one final thought. Attempting to be likable, like anything else, should be approached with a sense of balance. No matter what you do or how well you do it, you won't always be liked by everybody. As you experience more achievements, the number of people who dislike you will increase. Notice that I said the *number*, not the percentage, will increase. Ideally, the percentage of people who hold you in disfavor will remain low. However, with increased visibility and achievements, it is inevitable that the number of detractors will grow.

The hard fact is that people rarely take aim and shoot at a

person who is behind them. Usually, they fire at those they perceive to be out in front. Leaders are frequently the objects of rivalry and envy. Part of being a godly leader involves being thick-skinned enough to recognize and pray for others who struggle with jealousy.

Jesus' directives on how to treat our detractors come right to the point:

> But I say to you who hear, love your enemies, do good to those who hate you, bless those who curse you, pray for those who mistreat you . . . love your enemies, and do good, and lend, expecting nothing in return; and your reward will be great, and you will be sons of the Most High; for He Himself is kind to ungrateful and evil men. Be merciful, just as your Father is merciful.
>
> Luke 6:27, 28, 35, 36 NAS

It is hard for me to stay upset and angry at a person I'm praying for. Although our roles and functions may vary on a human level, in Christ we are all of equal value. No one is better than I am—and no one is worse. There is no pecking order. By remembering this, I can take less offense at criticism and feel less pride from praise.

The Apostle Paul tells us, "If possible, so far as it depends upon you, live peaceably with all" (Romans 12:18 RSV). The obvious point of this passage is to urge us to lead a peaceful coexistence with those around us. Yet it really blesses me that Paul began with that two-word phrase, "If possible." It is as if he realized that, no matter how hard we try, there will be some people we just cannot please. Over the years, in times of rejection, these words of Paul have encouraged me more than once.

KEY #6

God grants some individuals the gift (and awesome responsibility) of being leaders. To these people goes the solemn duty to apply Jesus' style of Servanthood Leadership. Simply put, this means leading others with one overwhelming goal: to better their lives and to enhance their fellowship with the Father.

A Christian leader sees the needs of others and realizes that they need him. This means becoming vulnerable. It requires being available. Ultimately, it means learning to lead other people by first learning to follow Jesus.

"Our heavenly father never takes anything from his children unless he means to give them something better."

—George Mueller

7

LEARNING TO
GIVE IT BACK

It had been a long trip. The missionary had visited all but one of his stateside supporters. This last visit was always his favorite. He loved to spend time with Mr. Jackson. This dear brother ran a large manufacturing firm, yet he always took time to hear about the missionary's work. When the missionary paid him a visit, Mr. Jackson would cancel his appointments and ask his secretary to hold all calls. He gloried in the missionary's exploits into the native villages. His eyes would moisten as the missionary told about the ones who had been saved. Mr. Jackson had a deep love for God's servants who ministered on the "front lines," as he put it. Near the end of the conversation, the businessman reached into his desk drawer and pulled out a personal checkbook. Silently he filled out one of the checks and tore it from the pad. Mr. Jackson had always been a generous Christian, but when the missionary glanced at the check he now held, he looked across the desk in astonishment. "This is a check for twenty-five thousand dollars! I never dreamed—"

"Just keep up the good work, brother. I love you," was the businessman's response.

The peacefulness of the moment was interrupted by the phone. As Mr. Jackson listened to the voice at the other end, his face became pale. "Are you sure?" he asked. "Is there any chance it can still be salvaged? Okay. Find out how bad it is and call me right back."

Out of concern, the missionary inquired what had happened.

"I was just notified that our largest client has canceled his contract with us. He represents over thirty percent of our business, and we have already expended millions of dollars in preproduction work for him. This may devastate our company," he explained somberly. "I'm going to have to ask you to give the check back."

"Sure," said the missionary, passing the check across the desk. "I understand."

Quietly, Mr. Jackson tore the check into several pieces and threw it away. Then he did a very unexpected thing. He reached into his desk drawer and pulled out the checkbook again. Without saying a word, he began to write out another check. When he was through, he slid it across the desk to his friend. The missionary looked at the check, then at Mr. Jackson. "What is the meaning of this?" he asked. "That phone call was terrible news, yet you have just given me a check for fifty thousand dollars! Why? You can't afford to do this."

"Brother, I can't afford *not* to," came the reply. "Right now, it's just between God and me—and I want Him to know where my trust is."

LEARNING TO GIVE IT BACK

One of the Most Important Lessons
We Can Learn

Mr. Jackson understood one of the most important lessons any Christian can learn. He had learned how to turn everything over to God—including his checkbook. Until God has control of our money, He really isn't our Master. Today, there are many Christians who know all the right answers. They sing beautiful praises. They study the Scriptures. They aren't shy about sharing their faith. They wouldn't dream of missing a worship service. But with it all, their hands are still tightly grasped around their wallets. These Christians have never learned what it means to really give of their wealth.

I am convinced that no Christian can enjoy all of the blessing God has in store for him until he learns how to bless others with his money. It is impossible to be fully successful without first developing this ability. But giving it away can be so hard to do. It means really trusting God to supply all of our needs. Maybe this is part of what Jesus had in mind when He told us, "If any man would come after me, let him deny himself and take up his cross daily and follow me" (Luke 9:23 RSV).

And the Devil Whispers . . .

Of course, the devil will fight us at every turn. He doesn't want us to relinquish our billfolds to God, so he tries to convince us that we really can't afford to give and that God doesn't care about what we do with "our" money. No matter what it takes, the devil is ready to do it to keep us from opening our purses to God. He wants us to analyze and legalize our giving. He loves to hear us debate questions like, "Is tithing required of Christians today?" and "Should I base my percentage of giving on my before-tax or my after-tax income?" and "Can I deduct essentials such as medical bills before I give to the Lord?" While these questions and others can be honestly and appropriately asked, far too often they tend to mask a deeper problem with the heart. Once we truly open our wallets to God, we'll find that we respond more to the needs before us than to some sort of legalistic formula.

The devil also tries to discourage us from giving by reminding us that sometimes undeserving people get the money. While we should be prudent and selective about whom we give to, there does come a time when we need to stop analyzing and start giving. This was brought home to me recently when a business associate shared something that had just happened to him. He told me he had stopped one afternoon to eat lunch at a fast-food Mexican restaurant. As he stood in line to place his order, a very simple, humble-looking man came up to the counter. He was dressed plainly and seemed a bit out of place in the surroundings. He asked the counter clerk what it would cost to buy a serving of sour cream to go with his meal. The clerk told him it would be twenty cents. The gentleman said, "Well, thank you anyway," and walked back to his table empty-handed.

My friend, seeing all of this, felt sorry for the man. He purchased an order of sour cream with his meal. As he passed the other man's table, he set the sour cream down beside him. The two men's eyes met for a moment. Nothing was said. To avoid embarrassing the gentleman, my friend walked to the other side of the restaurant and sat down. A few minutes later, he saw the man throw his papers into the trash and leave. That's when my associate got his surprise. That simple-looking man got into a brand-new Cadillac and drove off!

Although my friend shrugged the whole thing off, such an

occurrence would have depressed many of us. If our focus is wrong, an incident like this can cause us to become cynical and distrusting. The devil can use such an experience to convince us that we need to hold our money even more tightly. After all, how can we ever be sure the money we give will be used appropriately? Yet, for people like my business associate, this wasn't a problem because his focus was right. He didn't buy that sour cream for the man; he bought it for Jesus. His gift was given in faith. Jesus promises that nothing we give in His Name will go unnoticed (Matthew 25:31–46). When we adopt this attitude toward giving, the devil doesn't have a leg left to stand on.

Some Principles of Godly Giving

God is not silent on the subject of giving. There are a number of biblical teachings that will help us become the kind of givers He blesses. Let's take a few minutes and review some of these principles and the Scriptures that support them:

Principle #1: God expects us to give from our first fruits. Second best never has been and never will be good enough for God. He doesn't want our leftovers. God gave us His only Son; how can we afford to give Him less than our best? This was an early teaching of God to His people.

> Sanctify to Me every first-born, the first offspring of every womb among the sons of Israel, both of man and beast; it belongs to Me.
>
> Exodus 13:2 NAS

> You shall devote to the Lord the first offspring of every womb, and the first offspring of every beast that you own; the males belong to the Lord.
>
> Exodus 13:12 NAS

You shall not delay the offering from your harvest and your vintage. The first-born of your sons you shall give to Me. You shall do the same with your oxen and with your sheep. It shall be with its mother seven days; on the eighth day you shall give it to Me.

Exodus 22:29, 30 NAS

Now, I realize that some people will disagree with me on this, but I believe we should give to God before anything else comes out of our paychecks, no matter who we are indebted to, no matter how badly we need to buy groceries or anything else. God should come first. Proverbs 3:9 NAS gives us this directive: "Honor the Lord from your wealth, And from the first of all your produce." Then the writer completes this teaching with a beautiful promise in verse 10 NAS: "So your barns will be filled with plenty, And your vats will overflow with new wine." It seems God is promising us that if we put Him first in our giving, He will take care of our material needs.

Some Christians have found it helpful to establish a separate bank account that they refer to as their "First Fruits Account." By so doing, they are constantly reminded of whose money it really is. Additionally, it allows them to set aside the money they plan to give to God so it is always handy yet less likely to be spent on other things.

Principle #2: Giving should be a joyful experience. As a part of our worship of God, giving shows our love and praise. Accordingly, we should plan our giving in a thoughtful manner and rejoice at the privilege. In 2 Corinthians 9:7 NAS, Paul teaches, "Let each one do just as he has purposed in his heart; not grudgingly or under compulsion; for God loves a cheerful giver."

I wonder if God isn't a bit put off by some of today's high-pressure, coercive fund-raising techniques. His plan is for people to give because they want to give. I'm impressed by the way God encourages His followers to give from the heart. In Exodus 25:2 NAS, we hear God giving Moses an early lesson in fund-raising: ". . . raise a contribution for Me; from every man whose heart moves him you shall raise My contribution." Later, He speaks further on the matter: "Take from among you a contribution to the Lord; whoever is of a willing heart, let him bring it as the Lord's contribution: gold, silver, and bronze" (Exodus 35:5 NAS).

Apparently, it worked. Listen to what is recorded in the next chapter:

> And they received from Moses all the contributions which the sons of Israel had brought to perform the work in the construction of the sanctuary. And they still continued bringing to him freewill offerings every morning. . . . So Moses issued a command, and a proclamation was circulated throughout the camp, saying, "Let neither man nor woman any longer perform work for the contributions of the sanctuary." Thus the people were restrained from bringing any more. For the material they had was sufficient and more than enough for all the work, to perform it.
>
> Exodus 36:3, 6, 7 NAS

Isn't that interesting? God didn't tell Moses to bully, trick, or force. It appears the only gift God will accept must come from a loving and cheerful heart.

Principle #3: We should give as we have been gifted. God doesn't expect us to give what we don't have, but with blessings come responsibilities. In 1 Corinthians 16:2 NAS, Paul instructed each Christian to give based on his individual ability: "On the first day of every week let each one of you put aside and save, as he may prosper, that no collections be made when I come."

The amount that God expects you to give may be different from what He expects from me. The amounts and percentages will vary from one Christian to another. One servant may be led to give 10 percent, another 20 percent, and another 50 percent. One thing is constant: God expects all of His followers to have an open and abundant heart to His calling. As we submit ourselves to God and present ourselves as "living sacrifices" before Him, He will lead us and give us peace in this area.

God may lead some people to give up everything. We know at least one couple who feel the Lord led them to do just that. Over a dozen years ago, this couple felt that they needed to divest themselves of virtually all of their material possessions. They decided to get rid of the belongings that claimed so much of their time and energy. They sold their house and gave the proceeds to godly causes. After giving away much of what they had, they threw other items into the trunk of their car and drove it downtown. Finding a poor area of the city, they gave away its contents. In the years since that day, they have poured themselves out in ministry to people all over the globe. Through it all, God has faithfully provided for all of their physical needs: cars, clothes, money, even a house. He has never allowed them to be lacking.

A story like that makes me wonder what would have happened if the rich young ruler who came to Jesus had been willing to turn loose of his wealth (Matthew 19:16–26; Mark 10:17–30; Luke 18:18–30). Could Jesus have been testing him, much as God had tested Abraham to see if he was really willing to sacrifice his son, Isaac? (Genesis 22:1–19). Is it possible that Jesus might have rescinded His command had the rich man been willing to give it all up? Maybe such radical surgery would not have been necessary. Maybe God would have brought even greater blessings into his life, as he did for Abraham. We'll never know.

God requires different types of giving from different people. There is no glory in trying to fit into someone else's shoes. In chapter 1, we discussed the importance of finding and accepting God's special role for each of us. God asks for different gifts from different people. Some will be led to give predominantly on a financial level. Others may be led to sell some of their possessions for the Lord's work. This sort of giving is beautifully illustrated in Acts 4:32–37. Here we see the early Christians selling their possessions and donating the proceeds to help needy brothers and sisters.

Others may be called on to give of their time and talents. Recently, I went to Honduras to visit a Christian training center that our church is involved with. Illness and disease were everywhere, yet most of the people couldn't afford decent medical help. On the trip, I met two doctors and a nurse from the United States who were giving their time to treat suffering people in that Central American country. What a gift to Jesus! Instead of staying home and making money   enjoying a comfortable family vacation, they had chosen to invest their talents for God.

The Lord wants liberal hearts. He wants His people to happily give to meet the need. Paul reminds us of this in 2 Corinthians 9:6 NAS: "He who sows sparingly shall also reap sparingly; and he who sows bountifully shall also reap bountifully." Our giving, or lack of it, is a good test of our greed level. Jesus wants His followers to let go of everything, including their money.

A Crash Course in Godly Giving

This has been a hard lesson for me to learn. As a matter of fact, I'm still learning. One experience I'll never forget happened about a dozen years ago when the Lord decided to give me a crash course in the art of godly giving. At that time, Bonnie and I were relatively new in the business world. I suppose we had been far too conservative with our giving, so God used a visit from two missionaries to teach me an important lesson.

The two missionaries (one an old college friend of mine) asked if they could stay in our home while they were in Nashville to raise funds. At first I was delighted to have them, but as the days passed and their fund-raising proved unsuccessful, I became more and more uncomfortable with their presence. I became their biggest cheerleader. I *really* wanted them to raise that money so I wouldn't be put on the spot. They never put any pressure on me to give—but the Lord did. Clearly, if they were to get their money, it was going to have to come from us.

Finally, I realized that just like the rich young ruler, it was my time to put up or shut up. Did I really believe God could provide for all of our needs? Was I willing to take some of our security out of the bank and put it in God's hands? If my profession of faith was a serious one, it was time to come through with the physical evidence. Maybe this wouldn't have been a struggle for you, but it was for me. I found it very hard to let go, but with God's grace, I wrote out the check. It nearly stuck to my fingers as I handed it to them. The point is, I *did* hand it to them.

After the missionaries had received the money and left town, life went back to normal—or so I thought. It never occurred to me that God would respond to our gift the way

He did. In the next several weeks, it was as if God had opened the windows of heaven! We had an influx of blessings and new accounts that was totally unexpected. There was no rational explanation but to realize that God had honored our gift.

Over the years since that time, God has taught us a number of lessons about giving. Some have been painful. At times it has seemed as though God has had to take me to the woodshed to get my attention. Through it all, He has never let us down or allowed us to go wanting. Yet I still struggle with greed and selfishness. I don't trust God the way I want to. Too often, I hoard and covet. I still worry too much about tomorrow's provisions. But God isn't finished with me yet, and as I relinquish my will and my wealth to Him, He will replace it with His eternal wealth.

If you can relate to this, there is one final thought that might help you defeat the devil when he tempts you to withhold from God. The next time you are about to give an offering and the devil tempts you to cut back, play a little trick on him: give twice as much as you had planned to give.

Some Blessings of Godly Giving

One of the most powerful passages in the Old Testament is found in Malachi. Here we find God rebuking His people for not giving as they should. He tells them that this is robbery of God. Then He challenges them to get their priorities straight and test His generosity:

> "Will a man rob God? Yet you are robbing Me! But you say, 'How have we robbed Thee?' In tithes and contributions. You are cursed with a curse, for you are robbing Me, the whole nation of you! Bring the whole tithe into the store-

house, so that there may be food in My house, and test Me now in this," says the Lord of hosts, "if I will not open for you the windows of heaven, and pour out for you a blessing until there is no more need. Then I will rebuke the devourer for you, so that it may not destroy the fruits of the ground; nor will your vine in the field cast its grapes," says the Lord of hosts. "And all the nations will call you blessed, for you shall be a delightful land," says the Lord of hosts.

Malachi 3:8–12 NAS

To my knowledge, there is no place else in Scripture where God tells His people to test Him, but that's exactly what He is doing here. He promises the people three things if they give as they know they should. First, He guarantees He will open the windows of heaven and pour forth a blessing until there is no more need. Second, God tells them He will protect their crops from pestilence. Third, on a national level, He says other nations will honor them and there will be happiness within the nation.

Isn't that interesting? Apparently, if we put God first, He will care for us in return. Other passages throughout the Bible indicate the same thing:

How blessed is he who considers the helpless; The Lord will deliver him in a day of trouble. The Lord will protect him, and keep him alive, And he shall be called blessed upon the earth. . . .

Psalm 41: 1, 2 NAS

The generous man will be prosperous, And he who waters will himself be watered.

Proverbs 11:25 NAS

He who despises his neighbor sins, But happy is he who is gracious to the poor.

Proverbs 14:21 NAS

He who is gracious to a poor man lends to the Lord, And He will repay him for his good deed.

Proverbs 19:17 NAS

He who gives to the poor will never want, But he who shuts his eyes will have many curses.

Proverbs 28:27 NAS

Give, and it will be given to you; good measure, pressed down, shaken together, running over, they will pour into your lap. For whatever measure you deal out to others, it will be dealt to you in return.

Luke 6:38 NAS

Keeping Our Perspective

What a beautiful assurance. God will never let His people outgive Him! However, a word of balance is probably appropriate here. I'm sure you have heard some ministries ask for money and imply that the more you give the more you'll get. Some of these people have even gone so far as to put percentages of return on it. For instance, they may promise that "for every dollar you donate to the cause, God will repay you tenfold."

Like so much else about our walk with the Lord, giving is a matter of the heart. Just like the concept of grace, the concept of Christian giving can be easily misunderstood and misapplied. The intent can be easily counterfeited. We miss the point entirely when we give for the purpose of getting something in return. Our giving should be the ultimate form of selfless sharing, but like everything else we do for the Lord, the devil wants to pollute it. How better can he do this than by getting our hearts and motives turned selfishly inward? Our giving will gain its greatest blessing only when we do it from an unselfish heart.

The Freedom to Give

One of the greatest blessings of learning to give is the way it frees us from being slaves to our money. One can't be ruled by something he or she has given away. Agreed, there is no sin in having material blessings. The big question is, how are we using them? How well are we sharing with those who need our help? Again, the Bible gives us an important insight into this question:

> . . . Give me neither poverty nor riches; Feed me with the food that is my portion, Lest I be full and deny Thee and say, "Who is the Lord?" Or lest I be in want and steal, And profane the name of my God.
>
> Proverbs 30:8, 9 NAS

> "He who is faithful in a very little thing is faithful also in much; and he who is unrighteous in a very little thing is unrighteous also in much. If therefore you have not been faithful in the use of unrighteous mammon, who will entrust the true riches to you?"
>
> Luke 16:10, 11 NAS

There is another somewhat related blessing that comes from learning to give, but before we get to that, let's agree on one point: Most of the people who will read this book are rich. Now, you may not think of yourself as rich but if you own a car, have three pairs of shoes, and live in a heated home, you are rich by world standards.

Learning to give will help us relate to the poor and needy. Caring and giving to people who are hurting helps us empathize with them as human beings. Jesus was always very close to the poor. Somehow, I believe He was very comfortable visiting with street people. Reaching out to such people with our resources will bring us closer to the heart of Jesus.

When you come right down to the bottom line, none of us really owns anything. Accordingly, we are in error whenever we think of ourselves as masters. We are simply God's stewards, and we must be careful how we use the Master's possessions. God takes notice not only of what we give but also of what we have left. By adopting this attitude of stewardship we, like Paul, can say we have nothing yet possess all things (2 Corinthians 6:10).

"LIKE APPLES OF GOLD
IN SETTINGS OF SILVER
IS A WORD SPOKEN
IN RIGHT
CIRCUMSTANCES."
—PROVERBS 25:11 NAS

8

THE POSITIVE AFFIRMATION

Things had never come easy for Jake. Now he was thirty-five and the bank was about to foreclose on the family farm. His wife and two daughters would move with him to the city, where he hoped to find work. It was the night before the move. Most of their things were already on the old truck. As the family sat together on the porch, Jake couldn't help but think back over the years. There had been good times and hard times—especially hard times, the last two years in particular. Prices being paid for produce kept going lower and production prices kept going higher. In the last few months things had begun to get better. The trouble was, Jake just couldn't hang on any longer. The bank had run out of patience, and Jake had run out of time. If only he had another fifty thousand dollars, he could hold on until harvest. Then everything would work out.

As they all sat quietly on the porch, Jake pulled out his fiddle. He had never been a very good player, and it really didn't mean much to him. The only reason he had kept it was that it had been a gift from his father, who had died ten years earlier. Besides, the girls enjoyed hearing him squeak out an occasional tune. When he didn't have anything else to do, sometimes he would tune it up and perform for the family.

Tonight as Jake played the instrument, he felt a strange sense of bitterness. It was a feeling he'd had before. Why, he wondered, hadn't his dad left him something worthwhile? Instead he had inherited some broken-down equipment, a farm with a mortgage, and an old fiddle. When things were rough, his father used to find a lot of joy in playing that old fiddle. One time he'd even told Jake, "Son, whatever happens around here, this fiddle can lighten the load."

Lighten the load, Jake thought. *Music isn't going to lighten this load.*

Jake's life never did get much better. It was a series of menial jobs in different towns. The family sort of drifted apart. Jake always harbored the resentment toward his father. He was never really angry at his dad, but he frequently wished he had spent more time working the farm and less time messing around with that old fiddle.

It wasn't until after Jake died that the saddest chapter of his story was written. As a relative was boxing up his things, he ran across the old fiddle. Opening the case, out spilled an instrument the relative immediately recognized. This was no fiddle! It was a violin—an Italian instrument made in the 1600s by Giuseppe Guarneri! The instrument was worth much more than the fifty thousand dollars Jake had needed to save the farm—and his ruined life!

Like Jake, we often hold the solutions to our problems in our own hands and don't even realize it. How sad it is to spend a lifetime in defeat when it could be spent in victory! Yet much of mankind seems to live just such a muddled existence. So often, even those of us who have been saved fail to drink deeply of life's richest potential. In this chapter, I want to share a little secret of some of the happiest and most successful people I have ever known.

A Case in Point

Tim Pannell is one of the most successful young men I have ever met. Still in his twenties, he has racked up an extraordinary track record in the business world. After making a name for himself as a star salesman, he went into retailing, where again he produced a dazzling record. Today, Tim is a vital part of our organization. He wins more clients than anyone his age I've ever known. With it all, Tim is totally devoted to the truth and to playing by the rules. He is a Spirit-filled Christian, a committed husband, and one of the best fathers I've ever watched.

Recently, while on a trip together, I asked Tim to tell me his secret. I was interested to find out that it hadn't always been a bed of roses for him. There were some real tough times. Just like Moses, there was a wilderness period when he almost gave up in despair. A time when nothing made sense. A time when all his efforts ended in frustration and hopelessness. How did he turn it around? What happened to change things? I found Tim's story fascinating.

He told me how, six years ago, he had finally gotten to a point where he either had to fish or cut bait. Tim was at a crossroads. Despite numerous minor achievements, nothing was really coming together in his life. He was a Christian, but his walk was nonchalant. He had never really gotten off the fence between living the world's life-style and living the Lord's life-style. He was halfheartedly trying to serve two masters, and it just wasn't working.

Finally, Tim made a tough decision. He put himself on a 120-day mental diet. For those four months, he committed himself to a demanding daily discipline. His routine began each morning with a period of prayer and serious Bible study. Next, he went through his positive affirmation list (we'll go into more depth on this in a minute). Then he spent six to seven hours of the day listening to teaching tapes recorded by godly people. (Tim was selective in these tapes because his goal was to become a better servant of God—not, as he puts it, "just a humanistic, self-motivating machine.")

Prior to bed, he would spend time rereading all of his positive affirmation cards and then have another Bible study and prayer period. Psychologists tell us that what we feed our minds in the last minutes before sleep is what we are likely to dwell on and meditate on during the next eight hours. That is why it is so important to conclude the day with peaceful, holy thoughts. Bedtime isn't the time to watch the news or dwell on other stressful matters.

Today, Tim attributes that decision to turning his life around and giving it a purpose. It improved his self-discipline, blessed his business activities, and most of all brought him into a closer fellowship with God. Tim compares his mind with a garden he had spent over twenty years filling with whatever came along. He had allowed others to throw garbage into it. For his part, he hadn't spent much time cleaning or weeding it.

But cleaning and weeding wasn't all that needed to be done. Simply removing a negative situation doesn't solve very much if it isn't replaced by a positive solution. Notice this comment Jesus made, which sheds some light on this principle:

> Now when the unclean spirit goes out of a man, it passes through waterless places, seeking rest, and does not find it. Then it says, "I will return to my house from which I came"; and when it comes, it finds it unoccupied, swept, and put in order. Then it goes, and takes along with it seven other spirits more wicked than itself, and they go in and live there; and the last state of that man becomes worse than the first. That is the way it will also be with this evil generation.
>
> Matthew 12:43–45 NAS

Tim's 120-day purging allowed God to clean and weed the garden of his mind. But that wasn't the end of the process. Tim also busied himself with a plan to refill his heart and mind with the things of God.

To Narrow Our Focus

For the rest of this chapter, I want us to focus on one of the elements in Tim's daily routine: positive affirmation. This isn't to suggest that this one aspect was as important as the time he spent in prayer and study. It may not even have been as important as the time he spent with those training tapes. But if you are like many people, the concept of positive affirmation may be a new one.

I am aware that some Christians are troubled by the concept of positive affirmation. However, I do believe that there is an appropriate place for positive affirmation in the life of a Christian. I also believe that much of the problem is a semantical one. Before we go further, I want to take a few lines to explain what I *don't* mean by "positive affirmation."

I am most assuredly *not* referring to the attempts that secularists make to deny guilt in their own lives. The first step on the road to spiritual recovery is accepting personal blame for our sins and realizing that, without Jesus, there is no hope. I am also not referring to the mystical (even occult) incantations many in the unsaved world substitute for a saving faith in Christ. As you progress through this chapter, I trust you will find that my comments are grounded in the bedrock of the orthodox Christian faith.

To begin with, what is a positive affirmation? There is nothing mystical about it. It is simply a confident statement one makes for the future as if it were true in the present. It represents a goal one wants to achieve, or better solidify, in his or her life. At least one time every day, the individual repeats the positive affirmation to himself. As he repeats it, he thinks about what he is saying. He pictures himself that way.

For Example . . .

A very basic example of this is the positive affirmation I have started many mornings with for the last eighteen years: "I feel healthy; I feel happy; I feel terrific!" Now the fact is, many of those mornings I felt neither healthy nor happy, and I sure as shootin' didn't feel terrific. But I have found that by repeating this little phrase as though it were already true, it tended to actualize in my life.

To clarify further, let's look at some of the positive affirmations Tim continually repeated to himself for those 120 days:

- I am a hard worker.
- I am a good businessman.
- I am a loving individual.
- I am a joyful person.
- I am truthful.
- I am long-suffering.

- I am a meek individual.
- I am persistent.
- I am a good father.
- I am a peaceful person.
- I am a kind person.
- I am a gentle person.
- I am faithful.
- I am self-controlled.

These all began as goals that Tim wanted to achieve. As a matter of fact, he wasn't even a father when he began repeating these phrases, yet one of his positive affirmations was, "I am a good father." Why did he say that? Because he realized that one of the best ways to prepare for fatherhood was to build an inner awareness of its importance. He knew he would someday be a better father if he *believed* he was a good father. As one who has witnessed the way Tim relates to his two children today, I'd say his positive affirmation has paid off.

Overcoming Our Environment

The fact is that we live in a negative, fallen world. We all have friends who are in bondage to the devil. People around us are in pain. Every day, we work and deal with others who are depressed and disenchanted with life. The evening news is a kaleidoscope of pessimism. Much of our art and music reflects the unhappiness of its creators. Many of today's self-help articles sound like lessons in personal damage control. If there has ever been a time in history when positive affirmations were needed, it is now! We need to remind ourselves and those we love of the positive, righteous side of life. We need to focus our thoughts on the good. Every day a battle is waged to determine what will fill our minds that day. Will it be what is holy or what is common? Will it be what is clean or what is dirty? Will it be what lifts up or what tears down? It is our choice. Paul understood the importance of this:

> Finally, brethren, whatever is true, whatever is honorable, whatever is right, whatever is pure, whatever is lovely, whatever is of good repute, if there is any excellence and if anything worthy of praise, let your mind dwell on these things. The things you have learned and received and heard and seen in me, practice these things; and the God of peace shall be with you.
>
> Philippians 4:8, 9 NAS

One of the most effective ways to develop a belief system is to verbalize it. We tend to believe what we hear, even if it comes from our own mouths. Jesus referred to this critically important mind-to-mouth relationship when He spoke to a crowd of people one day: "Not what enters into the mouth defiles the man, but what proceeds out of the mouth, this defiles the man" (Matthew 15:11 NAS).

On the same point, James warned of the problems that come with misuse of the tongue. He made it very clear to the early church that the tongue is a powerful tool:

> So also the tongue is a small part of the body, and yet it boasts of great things. Behold, how great a forest is set aflame by such a small fire! And the tongue is a fire, the very world of iniquity; the tongue is set among our members as that which defiles the entire body, and sets on fire the course of our life, and is set on fire by hell. For every species of beasts and birds, of reptiles and creatures of the

sea, is tamed, and has been tamed by the human race. But no one can tame the tongue; it is a restless evil and full of deadly poison. With it we bless our Lord and Father; and with it we curse men . . . from the same mouth come both blessing and cursing. My brethren, these things ought not to be this way.

James 3:5–10 NAS

The Way of Grace

I believe it behooves those of us who want to experience godly success to realize the power our words hold. We should be very careful how we speak to ourselves. Yet frequently we are our own worst critics. I can still remember the times as a child when I would verbally assault myself after making a mistake on the ball field. Haven't there been times (lots of them) when you blew it, and you unloaded a verbal barrage on yourself that you wouldn't have tolerated from anyone else?

When you make a mistake, be gentle with yourself. Give yourself the benefit of the doubt. Don't talk too harshly to yourself. Maintain your sense of humor. Don't take yourself so seriously. Remember, the Bible tells you to "love your neighbor as yourself" (Leviticus 19:18 NAS). The implication we sometimes miss here is that God expects us to love ourselves. Without that self love, how can we love others? It's pretty hard to do, isn't it? Usually, we can't build others up without first knowing how to build ourselves up.

If you spend enough time pursuing a certain line of thought, whether it is good or bad, eventually it will affect your personality, attitudes, and environment. Although you may not be able to directly determine your environment, by carefully selecting your thoughts, you will indirectly determine that environment. This is why it is so important not to hit your head and call yourself "stupid" when you make a mistake. That seed of negativism will germinate in your subconscious. You will begin to believe and act that way.

Throughout Proverbs, the power of the tongue comes up time and again: "Anxiety in the heart of a man weighs it down, But a good word makes it glad" (12:25 NAS). "A soothing tongue is a tree of life, But perversion in it crushes the spirit" (15:4). "Pleasant words are a honeycomb, Sweet to the soul and healing to the bones" (16:24). "Death and life are in the power of the tongue, And those who love it will eat its fruit" (18:21). "Like apples of gold in settings of silver Is a word spoken in right circumstances" (25:11).

Broadening Our Concept

So far, most of our focus has been on making positive affirmations to oneself. Now, let's broaden that concept to include making positive affirmations to those we have contact with. Paul seemed to have this on his mind when he wrote to the Ephesians:

> Let no unwholesome word proceed from your mouth, but only such a word as is good for edification according to the need of the moment, that it may give grace to those who hear.
>
> Ephesians 4:29 NAS

God gives us numerous opportunities to brighten others' lives every week. Most of us function in at least three primary groups where positive affirmation will be helpful: our homes, the church, and the workplace. Let's take a moment and look at some ways we can be encouraging in each of these arenas.

Influencing Our Families With
Positive Affirmation

The first and most important sphere of influence for any-one (especially the husband) is the home. God expects us to build up and nurture our families in a special way. This is part of godly male leadership within the home. If a family member doesn't receive acceptance and approval from within the family, that person will either not develop a healthy self-esteem or he or she will look for it from others who may not share the same values.

The Bible has special instructions for fathers on this point: "And, fathers, do not provoke your children to anger; but bring them up in the discipline and instruction of the Lord" (Ephesians 6:4 NAS).

Notice also how husbands are exhorted by Peter (who was a married man) to be understanding and at peace with their wives:

> You husbands likewise, live with your wives in an under-standing way, as with a weaker vessel, since she is a woman; and grant her honor as a fellow-heir of the grace of life, so that your prayers may not be hindered.
>
> 1 Peter 3:7 NAS

So, great. Now that we know we are supposed to build self-esteem in our children and our wives, how do we do it? Not being a psychologist or a family counselor, I'm not qual-ified to go too far here, but one thing I know for sure is that fathers and husbands can bless their families by using lots of positive affirmations.

One of the highest goals for a godly woman is to please her husband. This puts a big responsibility on the man's shoulders to communicate his pleasure with her. There have been far too many evenings when I've returned home from work and not remembered this key point. Instead of starting the night with a few minutes of affection and kind words, my first comment to Bonnie has sounded more like, "Why's the house in such a mess?" or, "Weren't you going to get a plumber to fix the sink today?" This sort of behavior is totally insensitive to a woman's basic nature. It hurts her and puts her on the defensive.

More all the time, I'm trying to begin every evening with a positive affirmation like, "Wow, I really like the way you fixed your hair!" or, "Something smells great, what's for dinner?" or, "I'm really impressed by the job you have been doing on that committee."

Parents have a special responsibility to encourage their children. Without the encouragement of a thoughtful mother, life would have been very different for a small boy who grew up in Naples, Italy, in the late 1800s. His family was poor, yet he longed for the opportunity to learn to sing. Finally, when he was ten, he took his first voice lesson. "You can't sing. You haven't any voice at all," criticized his teacher. "Your voice sounds like the wind in the shutters."

The boy's mother, however, understood the power of positive affirmation. She believed her son had the talent to sing, and she told him so. She encouraged him to believe in himself. Putting her arms around him, she promised, "My boy, I'm going to make every sacrifice to pay for your voice lessons." Her confidence and constant encouragement paid off. By age twenty-nine, her son had acquired international fame. By the early 1900s, Enrico Caruso was widely considered the greatest operatic tenor of all time.

Parents owe their children a healthy self-image. It is vital that we be their biggest promoters. There will always be plenty of kids intent on telling them how fat, ugly, and dumb they are. There will be thoughtless adults who will make rude comments that will scar them as surely as acid etches glass. It is essential that we be their boosters.

I have learned that all three of our children are different. They are individual people with individual needs, goals, and interests. They are motivated and turned on in different ways. What works for one doesn't necessarily work for the others. Megan is more reserved than the other two. She appreciates beauty and art. Joshua is a thinker. He's always planning "inventions." Emilee is determined and tenacious. I'm sure you have heard of the pit bull. It is a breed of dog known for its toughness and determination. We call Emilee our pit baby.

With all of their differences, the children have one thing in common: All three of them become top performers when Mom and I build them up and encourage them. I am convinced that they will enjoy a happier, better-balanced adulthood if we speak words that picture a positive future for them. No matter how small an effort they make, they will work harder the next time if we show approval. We try to fill their little worlds with comments like, "God has given you a good mind. I'll bet you're going to do real well on that test next week," or, "Joshua, I was impressed by the way you opened the car door for Mother last night." I've noticed that each of the three respond differently to such comments, too. Usually, Megan just beams. Joshua (who's the talker) wants to discuss the comment and dwell on it. Emilee (who, you'll remember, charts her own course) is likely to respond to a complimentary comment with, "I know."

Another way I use positive affirmation with our children is after they are asleep. Psychiatrists still don't fully understand how our subconscious minds work, but it is my goal for our children to be thoroughly persuaded that they have been blessed with special talents and that God has important plans for them. When I go into their rooms to tuck them in at night, frequently I'll whisper positive affirmations into their ears. I say things like, "You're very special to God. He has a beautiful plan for your life," or, "Jesus loves you very much. One day you'll give your heart to Him," or, "Someday you'll get married. You're going to be a very good husband [wife]. You'll never get divorced. You'll always love your partner," or, "Mother and Daddy are glad God gave you to us to love," or, "You're going to have a happy life and then, one special day, you will go to live with God in heaven."

No, I don't know for sure if this works, but it surely can't hurt.

Influencing Our Church With Positive Affirmation

For me, one of the most interesting people in the New Testament is Barnabas. Some people think this is the Joseph called Barsabbas whom we first read about in Acts 1:23. The name *Barnabas* means, "consoler," or "one who encourages others." Acts 4:36 tells us the name *Barnabas* (which the apostles used for him) means "Son of Encouragement."

He may have gained the name *Barnabas* because of some consoling prophecy he delivered to the church in Jerusalem. At any rate, this early Christian must have exuded optimism. I believe he was the kind of a guy everyone liked to be around. He was a great servant of the church because of his ability to communicate trust and encouragement. When the newly converted Saul came to Jerusalem, he discovered that the Christians there thought he was a spy. It was Barnabas who encouraged them to trust and accept him (Acts 9:27).

Think about it: If it hadn't been for Barnabas' good word in his behalf, all of Paul's work and writings might never have materialized. Then in Acts 11:22–24, we are told that Barnabas was sent to the church in Antioch for the purpose of encouraging the Christians there.

Encouragement. It seems to be a fundamental principle of New Testament Christianity. In Romans 12:8, Paul lists exhortation as one of the seven spiritual gifts. I believe Paul was interested in seeing Christians become optimistic, encouraging, challenging people. This type of exhortation (encouragement) fills our hearts with the joy and exhilaration that comes from knowing Christ.

The writer of Hebrews speaks to this, too, in 10:24 KJV: "And let us consider one another to provoke unto love and to good works." I like the way he uses the word *provoke*. This is an aggressive word. It carries with it the idea of actively stirring others up or inciting them in a particular direction. As Christians, it mandates us to be catalysts for improvement in the lives of others.

Frequently, before we get out of the car at church, someone in the family will remind the others to "get your shakers out." With that, we all raise our right hands and shake them in the air. This reminds us that when we enter the building, we are there to shake hands and encourage others. Over the years, I've found that the more I ignore myself and get involved in encouraging other believers, the more I enjoy the fellowship.

There are always going to be people at church who are struggling and hurting. During any assembly, there will be some there who are bleeding inside. These people are desperately in need of having someone walk over, shake

hands, and inquire about them. They need to hear someone tell them that there is hope, that God loves them, that
God is aware of their trials, and that He really cares. They
need someone to hug them and pray with them (not *at*
them).

It is terribly inconsiderate for those of us who are enjoying
easy sailing to simply ignore these battered brothers and
sisters. Some of these souls have made a superhuman effort
just to come to church. They have come up for air for the
third time. If one of us doesn't reach out with compassion
and encouragement, these dear Christians may never come
back again. Maybe this is why God seems to put such a high
premium on being an encourager.

One of the greatest encouragers I have ever met is Walt
Leaver. We became friends in 1970, when he asked me to
serve on a freshman class committee with him. Even then,
Walt was well liked by everyone. There was an upbeat, enthusiastic air about him. Everyone he came in contact with
seemed to feel better. To this day, I still have the card he sent
me that Christmas. Even his card was encouraging (of
course, any card looks more lively when it is written with a
purple felt-tip marker pen).

Over the years, Walt and I have grown even closer. Today,
he preaches for one of the fastest-growing churches in middle Tennessee. In the sixteen years he has been there, the
congregation has grown more than 500 percent. Families are
being saved regularly. People are growing closer to Jesus
daily. Folks who have never found a happy church home
before are finding one where Walt preaches.

Why is all of this happening? Well, there are a lot of
reasons. Most important, God's hand has been with this
congregation. He has blessed the church with a devout
eldership. There are active youth, seniors, and singles min-

istries. There is an excellent staff. Although Walt would never mention it, the fact is, he is a vital part of the success formula. I am convinced that one of the reasons for the church's growth lies in Walt's personality. He is an encourager. He strives to build up others. When you are with Walt, you feel important. He helps others see and believe in their God-given talents. Walt has given his life over to others as a servant. He serves by being an encourager—a modern-day Barnabas.

Influencing Our Workplaces With Positive Affirmation

Most of the problems in the business world are people problems. Most of the losses the average company experiences are not caused by the economy, the competition, or the market. The vast majority of all setbacks can be directly attributed to employee dishonesty, incompetence, and low morale.

The big question is, what can be done to improve employee performance? Well, if you wade through several thick books and a half dozen business courses at the local college, you will probably come to this very simple conclusion: On the whole, people tend to perform and produce at just about the level you expect them to. If you think they are stupid, lazy, and dishonest, their performance will be stupid, lazy, and dishonest. But if you believe in them and treat them as if they are honest, hardworking professionals, that's what you'll get.

Over the years, I've seen a number of business operations. Frankly, I have never felt comfortable in a company where management kept the business offices locked up from the personnel, where some hawkeyed manager made rounds every six minutes to be sure no one was goofing off, or where there was an air of general distrust. Somehow, I can relax better in a more trusting atmosphere. I feel more at home in a company where there are no locked file cabinets in the building. The petty cash box is handy. There is no time clock. All the employees have keys to the door.

I prefer to be in a company where people are self-starters, where individual employees come and go as they wish, where everyone is a pro and performs like a pro.

How do you find such a gilded company? You make one!

If you are a company manager or owner, you have it within your power to make that firm just about anything you want it to be. In preceding chapters we discussed a number of helps in accomplishing this. Now let's briefly discuss one more: the positive affirmation.

Just as in the home and church, we can help people to vastly improve their job performance by helping them envision what they can accomplish. The best bosses I ever had were all back-patters. They rarely criticized my work. Instead, when my performance was weak, they encouraged me in alternate directions. When I showed improvement, they patted me on the back. Today, I try to follow that same policy. When I do so, the results are great. When I become a critic, performance deteriorates and morale evaporates.

Although I frequently fail, I try to remember that I should never make one negative comment to anyone if I haven't first made at least seven positive comments. Without first laying a positive foundation, I haven't earned the right to be negative. Now, you may be reading this and thinking about an employee whose thickest bone mass is between his ears. Maybe you are thinking, *Sure, that's all fine and good, but you don't know my employee, Bill Bonehead. It would take me a month to think up seven good things to say to him! In the meantime, he's making mistakes around here that hadn't been invented before I hired him.*

Before assuming the worst about your employee, take a personal inventory. Maybe this is a shortcoming on your side of the fence. You may need to ask God's help in looking for the good qualities in others. I have found that the more aware I am of my own faults, the more clearly I can see others' strengths. It is when I get to traveling along on my own ego trip that I tend to see the faults in others and miss their real assets.

As a final suggestion, you might want to put yourself on a plan of positive affirmations. As you shave, or drive to work, think about the employees you're most likely to see that day. Picture their faces, consider their individual needs, review their unique personalities. What sort of encouragement is appropriate? What would prove most helpful for each person? Then, plan a kind, truthful, encouraging comment for each one of them. Later, when you meet with them, pass them in the hall, or see them at their work stations, share your positive affirmations. Determine that you will stay on this regimen for thirty days. You may be surprised to find that you have developed a very pleasant habit by the end of the month.

KEY #8

To paraphrase Justin, "By examining the tongue of the patient, doctors determine the diseases of the body, and our friends the diseases of the heart." Make no mistake about it: our words have a powerful influence on others.

As James reminds us, we can use our words for good or bad, to bless or to curse, to build up or to tear down (James 3:1–12). A timely word of encouragement may be just the emotional plasma needed to lift the despair and dispel the fear that has another person in bondage. By cultivating a life-style of positive affirmation, we can affect the lives of those we love throughout eternity.

"ONE OF THE GRANDEST GIFTS WE CAN GIVE THOSE WE LOVE IS A SWEET MEMORY."

9

BUILDING MEMORIES

I can still see him. Complete with his fur-lined red suit and white beard, it was none other than Santa Claus! In the flesh—coming into my house! Sure, all the other kids had seen him in the department stores, but not a single one of them could say that Santa had come to his or her home for a personal visit just before he began his worldwide flight.

Somehow, this famous man in red made a habit of showing up at our home right at bedtime on Christmas Eve for a number of years in the late 1950s. I remember jumping into his lap, loving on him, and making doubly sure that he was coming back later in the night with some of the toys I had discussed in my letter. Then he would open his sack, pull out some suckers for my sisters and me, and leave nearly as fast as he had arrived.

It wasn't until some years later that my father filled in all the details. He explained that, for a few dollars, he had hired the Santa Claus at Loveman's Department Store to drop by our home and fill our little minds with the enchantment only a child can understand. He explained that his own father had begun this tradition with him by dressing up as Santa and visiting my dad as a boy. Probably more than anyone else I have ever known, my father understood the importance of being a memory builder.

Although Christmas was an especially important time during my boyhood, Dad was profoundly dedicated to building memories on a year-round basis. He had a way of turning a fishing trip, or a roadside picnic on a summer afternoon, into a memory. As far as Dad was concerned, a paved driveway was not living up to its full potential until there was a shuffleboard court painted on it. He could hardly wait until I was out of school in the summer so we could travel together as he visited clients. My father understood the essence of turning otherwise insignificant occurrences into unforgettable events.

Dad was a man who had a keen appreciation for tradition. He instinctively understood the role such traditions play in forging a child's sense of self-worth and importance. For him, categorical success included raising balanced, emotionally well-adjusted children. To that end, he believed every kid needed a rich background of happy memories that could be stored away like preserved fruits. Later, when the inevitable dark days of winter came, they could be served up to brighten an otherwise gloomy day. Dad understood the emotional insulation a sweet memory could represent when dealing with a bitter outside world.

It should come as no surprise to anyone who knows my background that I am totally satisfied that a heritage of memories is one of the most important elements to success and real happiness. Whether you are attempting to manage a business, lead a church, or raise a family, you will find that having your own traditions will build morale and a sense of purpose like few other services you can render.

Becoming a Memory Builder at Home

Now, if all of this seems foreign to you, be patient. Being a memory builder is not only simple, it is also a lot of fun. As a matter of fact, all it takes is a little ingenuity and planning.

Bonnie and I have always tried to bless our kiddos with lots of sweet memories. Vacations are planned with the children in mind. We avoid frequent nighttime meetings if the children aren't invited. My favorite golfing and fishing buddies are our kids. Frequently, the whole family will spend part of the evening in Mom and Dad's bed enjoying snacks, TV, or board games.

We made the decision four years ago to home school our children. Undoubtedly this is a new concept to many people, and it is not my purpose here to argue the merits of parents teaching their children at home. However, this practice has brought our family together more closely than anything else we could have done. Bonnie isn't only Mom, she's also their teacher. This decision has given the children countless experiences with Bonnie that they never would have enjoyed otherwise. Learning to read from their mother, cultural tours to the museum, nature hikes, and field trips—all in all, it has caused an unusually strong bond to form. We believe it will make them more capable and stable adults.

One of my memory-building traditions with the children has drawn some raised eyebrows from other adults, but the kids love it and I'm not about to quit. It's sort of like the old midnight refrigerator raid—intensified. Here's how it works:

Occasionally, late on a nonschool night, I'll wake up one of the children so we can "sneak" out of the house for a snack. (I've found that using the word *sneak* adds an extra dimension of excitement and intrigue.) We get dressed and quietly slip out to the car. Then we head for that child's favorite all-night eatery. Once there, anything goes! Ice cream, doughnuts, hamburgers and fries—it doesn't matter. This is our special "secret" nighttime fling.

On one such occasion, when Megan was about six, we had gone to an all-night ice cream shop. With absolutely no regard for calories, I had ordered a large sundae. Just as I was about to eat the first bite, Megan looked across the table and said softly, "Daddy, some people think you're fat, but I don't." Needless to say, she curbed my appetite that night!

Now, I know what you might be thinking. This is no way to bring up children. It's not good for them to miss their rest and eat at night. So far, it hasn't done any harm, and the memories are worth it all.

Often we build memories without even trying to do so. Recently, we had gone out to eat at one of the kids' favorite restaurants after church. Of course, no family outing is complete without the obligatory trip to the rest room. About five minutes into the meal, I found myself taking Joshua, our six-year-old, to the little room at the end of the hall. When we were ready to leave, as I held the door for him, the little fellow looked up at me and said, "I know why you want to open the door for me. It's so when you're an old man, you can think back about what a good time we're having here tonight."

To be truthful, until that moment, I was unaware that we were having such a good time. In his own way, Joshua helped me remember that we are always making memories.

It's just a question of whether they will be good ones or bad ones.

Bonnie has brought sparkles into our lives with her memory making, too. I'll never forget the surprise she had waiting for me on our twelfth wedding anniversary. Everybody knew about it but me.

Bonnie got the creative staff at the office to help her with the deception. They told me they had scheduled a photo shoot at our church building. It seemed odd, but with straight faces they explained that it was for a magazine layout. They went on to tell me I had to be involved. This, too, seemed unusual, but I swallowed the whole story.

When I arrived at the building, there was no company van, no photographer, no assistant, no model, so I went to the church office to find out what was going on. The secretaries just giggled and handed me a note. It told me to go to one of the classrooms. Obediently, I found the room and went in. My tuxedo was laying on the table next to a lapel rose. The note told me to put it on and come to the auditorium. By now I knew I'd been had, but I was too curious not to play along.

A few minutes later, I reported to the auditorium in my tux. As I entered, I noticed the lights were dimmed. I instinctively looked to the front. There, like a dream, stood my bride in her wedding gown. In the next few precious minutes we drank fruit juice from our wedding goblets and looked at our picture album as the tape recording of our wedding service played.

Bonnie had the whole night planned. A few moments later, a long, white limousine swept up to the door and took us away to our favorite French restaurant. That was followed by a trip to a beautiful resort hotel, where we spent the night. Now, folks, that's a memory!

Building Memories at Work

Let's shift our focus to memory building in the business arena. We have built a lot of them over the years in the business. Obviously, traditions that have served us well may not fit your circumstances at all, but maybe our traditions will serve as thought sparklers for you.

When we officially opened our doors for business in May 1977, it was just Bonnie and myself. We had a meager suite of three offices on Music Row in Nashville. Bonnie was our receptionist, secretary, and office manager. I was the sole account executive, coypwriter, media buyer, television producer, artist, and general flunky. By December, we had two other employees. Six employees and spouses enjoyed the first annual Steve Diggs & Friends Advertising Agency Christmas dinner. We were such a small group that the waitress was able to seat us in a corner booth at the restaurant.

As the years passed (and our numbers grew), the Christmas dinner became a company fixture. As a matter of fact, it was so popular that we added another dinner in May of each year to celebrate our company anniversary. To this day, a typical evening may begin with dinner at a nice restaurant. Then everyone will go to one of our homes for dessert and fellowship. One of the popular events of the evening is perusing a company scrapbook I have kept from our earliest days. It is filled with old staff and party photos, press clippings, ad campaigns, and so forth. This book is of inestimable importance to the company's overall sense of cohesion.

Of course, we have always made it a point to be more than associates in the workplace. We really do cherish one another's friendship. To that end, we like to socialize with one another. Whether it is a picnic at one of our homes, a whitewater rafting trip, a fishing expedition, a wedding or baby shower, or our annual softball game, we have found that the best business relationships really can be among friends.

Another tradition that dates back to our earliest days is the Monday Morning Devotional & Staff Meeting for our management team. From the first day of business, we dedicated the firm to God. It isn't my business—it's His. Over the years, we have always tried to remember that all we have is a gift from God. He has been our strength through numerous challenges. He is the One who has always given the increase. To that end, we feel it is appropriate to begin the work week in worship. On Monday morning at 7:30 A.M., we open the week with songs, a prayer, and a reading from Scripture.

Only then do we start our business activities. It is amazing how God has honored these devotions. We have learned that our heads are clearer for business when our hearts are focused on God.

One last company tradition that has proved a real blessing over the years is our annual Christmas family. Our staff believes that Christians should contribute from all of their resources. This means if you are involved with a business, that business should be used to serve the needs of others.

Every holiday season, one of our staff members locates a family in the community that is experiencing hard times. We get all the pertinent information about sizes, ages, and preferences. Then everyone goes to work to be certain our family experiences a royal Christmas, complete with a visit from Santa Claus, loads of toys, and enough food and clothes to last well into the winter. It requires some extra effort, but everyone in our firm will tell you that we are really the ones who receive the greatest blessing from this event.

Memories (or, if you wish, traditions) are the building blocks of any solid organization. They are an essential part of an organization's culture. Whether it is a family, church, business, or club, nothing else does more to promote a sense of security and well-being.

Back to the Man Who Taught Me All I Know

Earlier in this chapter, I shared with you some of the memories my father built for us. It is amazing to me how God blessed Dad in return. In the twelve months from June 1985 to June 1986, God blessed Dad with a wealth of memories that neither he nor the rest of us would ever forget. It was almost as if God had said, "Herbert Diggs, you have spent a lifetime building memories for others—now it's your turn." In that twelve-month span, Dad enjoyed one precious memory after another. It began on June 7, 1985, when I received a letter from my father:

> Dear Steve,
> Son, our ship came in yesterday. We're still pinching our-selves and trying to believe it. It was better than expected and more is due on or soon after July 2, 1985. . . .

With that introduction, Dad went on to tell me that he and Mother had received a completely unexpected windfall income that would allow them a lot more free time.

As the months passed, more wonderful things happened. My father's schedule developed so that it allowed Mother and him more time together than they had ever had before. They spent their days reminiscing about the past and dreaming of the future. Their evenings were relaxed and comfortable. They were both with their best friend.

The apples of his eye were Dad's grandkids. During this period, he had an unprecedented amount of time with each of them. He spent countless hours rolling on the floor with the grandkids, splashing them in the little backyard pool, taking walks with them, and enjoying the Thanksgiving and Christmas holidays together. Dad thought every kid needed an endless supply of bubble gum, so they were always running to the store to get another pack of Bazooka.

During those twelve months, Dad and I had a number of opportunities to be together and communicate with one another on a soul level. In April 1986, he spent an entire day with me at the office and going about my daily routine. It reminded me of all the times I had gone to work with him when I was young. It was wonderful, but somehow hauntingly strange, that now he was coming with me. I remember noticing how tired he looked that day.

We also had an opportunity to travel together and really get to know each other better than ever before. I remember our conversation that night as we drove back home. We talked about our spiritual values, our assurance of heaven, and our common faith in Jesus. In May 1986, my parents visited us in Nashville. Dad, my son, Joshua, and I spent a Saturday afternoon fishing and picnicking.

During that year, we spent a lot of time together talking and building memories. However, there are two days that stand out over all the rest. If I live to be a hundred years old, I will never forget two days in June 1986. On the evening of June 20, we had arrived in Oak Ridge to visit my folks for the weekend. For some reason, I really wanted to spend some time alone with Dad that night. After dinner, I suggested that the two of us go for a drive. One thing led to another and before we knew it, we were at Pigeon Forge, a resort town nearly fifty miles away. By this time it was after midnight, but we didn't let that deter us. We stopped long enough to do some (are you ready for this?) go-cart racing.

On the way home, we stopped at an all-night diner in Knox-ville for Coney Island hot dogs.

The next day was a happy one. We visited and talked about the things dads and sons discuss. In the afternoon, Dad enjoyed watching the children splash in the pool. He nearly fell out of his chair when Joshua decided to spray me down with the hose. As the evening neared, Dad started the grill in anticipation of a family dinner as he had done so many times before. That's when it happened.

I was in the house when my sister Sharon came rushing in from the backyard screaming, "Hurry! Call an ambulance!" I rushed out and looked down to the patio below the porch. My dad was lying unconscious on the concrete. I rushed down to him. A moment later, Bonnie was with me. To-gether we began to apply CPR.

In the next minutes, a very happy day turned unspeakably sad. We went to bed that night without our father. Two days later, I preached the funeral.

As I prepared my comments for the funeral, I began to see God's hand in all the events of the past year. What a blessed year He had given my father—and all of us. In His own way, God had cushioned the blow by allowing my father to build some of our most important memories in the last hours of his life.

Deep within each heart is the need for a bridge from the past to the present. Maybe it is based on a desire we have to identify our roots. Maybe it comes from the gut-level cognizance we all have of the eternal. I'll leave that debate for the psychologists and the philosophers. All I know is that this soul-deep need exists in all of us. It is only with such a link to the past that we can fully maximize the present.

In their landmark book, *Love Is a Choice*, doctors Robert Hemfelt, Frank Minirth, and Paul Meier discuss codependency in a refreshingly concise manner. One point they develop is the "love tank" concept. They encourage the reader to imagine being an infant possessing a heart-shaped love tank. They explain that the love tank is nearly empty at birth. It is the parents' job to fill the child's love tank.

Being more of a pragmatist than a theoretician, I can really relate to what the good doctors are saying. One of the best ways to fill a child's love tank is with a sweet memory or a family tradition. It doesn't require wealth, a college education, or any professional credentials. All it requires is a selfless, Christlike love that takes the necessary time to build a memory and fill a love tank.

Whether it is with our children and spouses or those with whom we work or worship, there is no better way to bless another person than with the construction of a happy memory.

"TIME: A GIFT GIVEN EQUALLY TO ALL BY THE FATHER."

10

MANAGING YOUR
VANISHING INVENTORY

In the broadcasting business, advertising time slots on radio and television are sometimes referred to as the "vanishing inventory." This is because any commercial time slots that are not sold to advertisers before they roll around will vanish forever, never to be available again. Thus, unlike newspapers, to which pages can be added or deleted based on the number of ads sold in any given issue, radio and TV stations will often offer unsold time slots at the last minute at sharply reduced prices.

Unfortunately, we, too, live in a "vanishing inventory" world. We have a very finite amount of time available to us, and it is our job to maximize the time we have been given.

The good news is that we all start on a level footing in this arena. No one, no matter how rich or smart or powerful he or she is, has one more minute of time in his day than you have in your day. You have something in common with Ross Perot, Lee Iacocca, George Bush, and Sam Walton! Your day yesterday had the same twenty-four hours in it as their day.

The real question is this: Did you invest your time as efficiently yesterday as they invested their time? Or did you end the day somewhat frustrated and a little overwhelmed by a work load that exceeded your time allotment?

There is an allegory told about a father who gave his son $86,400 to be spent any way he chose. The only stipulation was that the boy had to spend all of the money in one day. If anything was left over, it would have to be returned to the father. In much the same way, our Heavenly Father has allotted to each of us 86,400 seconds every single day. We begin every morning with all the hope and potential of that day's 86,400 seconds. What we do with each of those seconds will determine whether that day is a success or a failure.

In a metaphor Paul borrowed from merchants who happily parted with their pleasures and painstakingly prepared for their business day, when they would be busy buying and selling, he said, "See then that you walk circumspectly, not as fools but as wise, redeeming the time, because the days are evil" (Ephesians 5:15, 16 NKJV).

I really like the way Paul selected the word *redeeming*. It carries with it the idea of being able to repurchase something or change it for the better. In a very real way, that is exactly what God expects us to do with the time He has given us: exchange it for something of even greater value.

How do we accomplish this? How do we make the most of the time God has given us? How do we invest our time in other people's lives, our jobs, and our ministries to the fullest?

A Two-Step Approach

There are two amazingly simple ingredients involved in redeeming the time we have been given. The first is to work hard. The second is to work smart. Pretty basic stuff, right? Then why are there so many folks out there who constantly have more tasks than time? I believe it is because very few of us have ever stopped and really pondered the nature of the problem. With your indulgence, we're going to briefly explore these two ingredients of successful time management.

First, let's consider the concept of working hard. Solomon's advice in Ecclesiastes 9:10 NIV cuts right to the heart of the matter: "Whatever your hand finds to do, do it with all your might, for in the grave, where you are going, there is neither working nor planning nor knowledge nor wisdom."

Unfortunately, it doesn't always work this way. One of the most disappointing lessons I have learned in my years in the business world is that the vast majority of people in the marketplace are content with mediocrity. Some people seem satisfied delivering the lowest level of service possible to maintain their jobs. Instead of jobs, these people want "positions." The sad fact is, frequently people are not willing to do what it takes to earn those desired positions.

We once hired an individual who had just graduated from college with a degree in advertising. Fred (not the person's real name) had been unsuccessful in locating a job elsewhere. He was referred to me by a mutual friend.

From the start, it was obvious that Fred lacked the dedication and work habits necessary to succeed in the marketplace. He wanted a title, but he simply wasn't willing to put out the effort to earn it. For some time, we lived with the situation. The real shock came one day when I met Fred's father. Without asking about Fred's performance or attitude, he was critical of me for not paying Fred more money. I fought the temptation to tell him the reason Fred wasn't being paid more and held my tongue.

It wasn't long before Fred quit. To my knowledge, he never has found a job in advertising. Fred's problem wasn't that he didn't have an education, and it wasn't that we didn't give him an opportunity to perform. Fred's problem was himself. He wasn't willing to do what it took to win.

Contrast this "work ethic" of many today to the teachings of Scripture:

> Go to the ant, O sluggard, Observe her ways and be wise, Which, having no chief, Officer or ruler, Prepares her food in the summer, And gathers her provision in the harvest. How long will you lie down, O sluggard? When will you arise from your sleep? "A little sleep, a little slumber, A little folding of the hands to rest"—and your poverty will come in like a vagabond, And your need like an armed man.
>
> Proverbs 6:6–11 NAS

> The soul of the sluggard craves and gets nothing, But the soul of the diligent is made fat.
>
> Proverbs 13:4 NAS

What is the biblical response to such behavior patterns? We can get some insight into this matter by looking at Paul's teaching to a group of Christians in Thessalonica who had abandoned their jobs:

> For you yourselves know how you ought to follow our example, because we did not act in an undisciplined manner among you, nor did we eat anyone's bread without paying for it, but with labor and hardship we kept working

night and day so that we might not be a burden to any of you; not because we do not have the right to this, but in order to offer ourselves as a model for you, that you might follow our example. For even when we were with you, we used to give you this order: *if anyone will not work, neither let him eat.* For we hear that some among you are leading an undisciplined life, doing no work at all, but acting like busybodies. Now such persons we command and exhort in the Lord Jesus Christ to work in quiet fashion and eat their own bread.

2 Thessalonians 3:7–12 NAS, my italics

Your Personal Best

An example of such diligence can be seen in almost any restaurant. You can usually spot the owner or manager within a couple of minutes. He's the guy who is running at full speed, making sure each customer has the right order, ringing patrons out at the cash register, and busing tables— all while the other employees wander around looking for something to do.

You see, the owner is motivated to do the best he can because it is his business and he sees the big picture. He clearly understands the link between delivering a quality product and making a profit. On the other hand, many of his employees suffer from tunnel vision. It's just a job to them. As far as most of them are concerned, the paycheck is the same whether they put out 10 percent or 100 percent. Very few realize that if that restaurant fails to deliver a superior product, the customers will soon go elsewhere—and when the customers stop coming in, it won't be long before there are no more jobs.

If you are not happy with your present job, there are two ways to solve your problem: One, you can deliver substandard work to your employer until your services are no longer required. Two, you can deliver such consistently superior work that your employer realizes he can no longer succeed without you. This second approach will eventually lead to advancements and opportunities that will propel you from your present position to increasingly better ones.

One of the first things I tell people who want to excel is to forget the forty-hour-week myth. I don't apologize for this. There is virtually no such thing as becoming a peak performer in the business or ministerial world by working only a forty-hour week. If you are not prepared to dedicate yourself more than the average worker, you will never receive more than the average return.

Diligence vs. Workaholism

This is not an attempt to excuse the excessive workaholic type. Granted, there are many people in our society who believe it is almost a badge of honor to be called a workaholic. I was once told of a young executive who regularly arrived at the office at two o'clock in the morning! There are many businessmen who neglect their wives and children to move up the corporate ladder.

This sort of thing is foolish and sinful. The price is far too great. Something will break if it goes on very long. It may be your spiritual walk, your family relationships, your health, or all three. I know. I am a recovering workaholic. I'm not proud to admit that fact, but it's true. In our earlier years, I worked plenty of ninety- to one-hundred-hour weeks. Even when my body was at home, my mind was still at work. It took two trips to the hospital to get my attention.

Before we go any further, I need to put a warning label on what I'm about to say. You may want to think of this as the skull and crossbones for the rest of this section. If you are a driven, overambitious individual, just ignore what I will be saying about working hard—it's not for you. If you are already putting in seventy-hour weeks, this will be like pouring gasoline on a flaming fire. You don't need to work harder, you need to calm down and slow down! You need to regain a balanced existence. There is a place where virtue becomes vice, where toil becomes excessive.

An inordinate work schedule is wrong. Too many Christians in our society have allowed legitimate diligence to become vain striving. In Psalm 127:2 NAS, the writer says it this way: "It is vain for you to rise up early, To retire late, To eat the bread of painful labors; For He gives to His beloved even in his sleep." Remember, when you strip all the fat from the bone, our only real purpose for being here is to glorify God and share the saving news of Jesus with others. When our work schedules cease to do this, it is best to cease our work.

Time management, like so many other spheres of involvement, requires a sense of balance. Somewhere between the seventy-hour-a-week workaholic and the thirty-hour-a-week goofaholic is the truth. One simply cannot establish a successful clientele, ministry, business, or practice by working no more than what would be expected from an employee. Although it will vary from individual to individual, it is probably safe to advise anyone considering opening his or her own business to plan to average forty-five- to fifty-five-hour weeks for at least the first couple of years.

Additionally, these first intensive years are no time to be taking extended vacations. With the exception of an occasional long weekend trip, you will probably have neither the time nor the discretionary funds for recreational travel. It will require this kind of consistent concentration and dedication to really succeed in our competitive marketplace.

I realize that this may sound like a lot to ask of anyone. Over the years, I have learned not to push people on this issue. Winning businesses are built by people who are goal-oriented, focused on the task, and self-disciplined enough not to waste time looking for shortcuts and "get rich quick" schemes. The most successful people in the world are those individuals who do the same right thing every day. Granted, it can get monotonous, and often it isn't very glamorous, but this path of dogged consistency is the surest route to success and happiness in any realm.

This lesson was brought home to me by an individual I have observed for the last eighteen years. Ever since our first meeting, William (his real name and certain details have been changed) has dreamed of accomplishing great things in the professional world. He has held at least ten jobs since college graduation. Yet, to my knowledge, he has never really enjoyed long-term success at any of those jobs. It is because William is a victim of his own deadly triangle. On one side, he has always had a "get rich quick" mentality. He has wasted untold amounts of time and money trying to find a shortcut to the rainbow's end—so far, without success.

The second side of his triangle is a drive for prestige. He has always invested a lot of effort trying to be perceived by others as a success. Over the years, he has frequently made a wonderful first impression on people, only to disappoint them at a later time.

The third side is equally deadly. William has fastidiously refused to invest the effort necessary to enjoy the success he wants to achieve. One of his typical workdays might not begin until late morning, only to end with a midafternoon golf game.

To succeed in any endeavor, a person must be willing to pay the dues and work the hours. To perform at top potential, you have to be a self-starter.

Self-Discipline: A Personal Decision

Like anything else, you have to know where the cutoff valve is and when to use it. In other words, you must know when the organization has reached a self-sustaining level that allows you to cut back on your hours. Many people who worked hard in the early years out of necessity never get around to slowing down. Again, we must remember that God doesn't define *success* as the accumulation of wealth. He defines it as walking closely and uprightly before Him. It is important to see the first two- or three-year period as temporary, not a permanent life-style. Your plan should be to work extra hard for a short period of time in order to have more discretionary time later. Ideally, much of this discretionary time will be invested in your family and your ministry before God. After all, the goal should be to become continually more freed from worldly entanglements and more able to serve God.

One other pitfall that otherwise successful people often fall into is the trap of buying things they don't need and really can't afford. I don't want to digress too far here, but a word of caution is in order. It is very easy to become dazzled by the first profits you earn. These early profits need to be used wisely. The first fruits should always go back to God, and most of the rest should be reinvested in conservative ways. This money doesn't need to be spent on country club memberships, extra cars, fancy homes with big mortgages, expensive clothing, and other high-profile luxuries.

How Much Will Be Enough?

As a matter of fact, one of the decisions that should be made early is, how much will be enough? Think about it for a minute. Suppose you were to be blessed with a financially successful business. How much would it take to satisfy you? How many cars would it require? What size home? Would it have to have a swimming pool for you to be happy? How about clothes—would you have to wear the most expensive suits to be happy? Would you constantly be looking for longer and more extravagant vacations? If these are the things you are striving for, it is time to push the "hold button."

Let me encourage you to prayfully consider ways not to become dazzled by this world's counterfeit status symbols. There will always be something bigger, flashier, and more expensive. There will always be a tension between proper stewardship and godless materialism. Determine early how much will be enough, then stick to that decision, even if God blesses you with great material gain.

Learning to Work Smart

The second ingredient that is required to effectively redeem our time is the ability to work smart. Agreed, an individual must be willing to work hard, but if that is all he does, he will succeed only at kicking up a lot of dust.

Working smart means being a thinker. It means having clear goals and time schedules. In order to remember your goals and maintain your schedule, it is wise to write them down. This will help you *preact* to the events of the day instead of having to *react* to them. Without a clearly planned schedule, your time will be spent dealing with problems rather than opportunities.

I advise keeping two lists. One should be your "Daily Things to Do" list and the other should be a list of long-term goals.

Your next day's "Things to Do" list should always be the last thing you do before going home in the evening. I realize that some people suggest preparing this list early in the morning, but I have found that if I wait to do it in the morning, it is easy for me to forget pressing things from the day before. Additionally, it is good motivation for me to get out of bed on time if I know exactly what my first task of the day is going to be.

John Ruskin, British art critic, is reported to have had a small block of marble on his desk with the word *Today* chiseled into it. This was a reminder to him that there was no place in his world for procrastination. He meant to do that day's jobs that day.

The "Things to Do" list should be prepared in the order one plans to perform the tasks. It is always wise to start with the most urgent and least enjoyable jobs. If there is an especially annoying chore, a mundane project to finish, or an unpleasant phone call to return, I've found it best to tackle that job within the first thirty minutes after arriving at work. This way, as the day progresses, it gets better and better, and I don't find myself dreading a job I have put off.

One of the greatest benefits of such a list is the way it helps me accomplish more in the course of a day. By remaining focused, I don't waste time looking for something to do. I become more punctual. Being late to appointments is less of a problem. Remember, when one sets an appointment, he or she assumes the responsibility of punctuality. That individual does not have the right to be a single minute late.

As you use your "vanishing inventory" more and more wisely, you will find that it takes less time to do the same amount of work. It is like comparing a small wheel with a large wheel. The small wheel travels a very short distance with each revolution, while with each revolution the more efficient large wheel goes much farther. By becoming increasingly more efficient, you will be surprised by your own achievements.

Preparing Your List of Long-Term Goals

Your second list should be long-term goals. This will become your master plan. The items on this list should be the product of serious prayer and meditation. If we want to enjoy God's best for our lives, we must first seek His counsel. James tells us, "But if any of you lacks wisdom, let him ask of God, who gives to all men generously and without reproach, and it will be given to him" (James 1:5 NAS).

God has always wanted His people to come to Him for wisdom and discernment. He wants us to look to Him for direction in our lives. Like any father, God really wants to be close to His children and involved in their daily activities. One of the most blessed individuals in all of history was King Solomon. All of his blessings of riches and honor came from the basic understanding he had that God was the exclusive Source of the wisdom and purpose in his life.

The account of how Solomon received these gifts from God is one of the most interesting stories in Scripture. It gives us a glimpse into how God thinks and where He wants us to put our priorities:

In Gibeon the Lord appeared to Solomon in a dream at
night; and God said, "Ask what you wish me to give you."
Then Solomon said, ". . . And now, O Lord my God,
Thou hast made Thy servant king in place of my father
David; yet I am but a little child: I do not know how to go
out or come in. . . . So give Thy servant an understanding
heart to judge Thy people to discern between good and
evil. For who is able to judge this great people of Thine?"
And it was pleasing in the sight of the Lord that Solomon
had asked this thing. And God said to him, "Because you
have asked this thing and have not asked for yourself long
life, nor have asked riches for yourself, nor have you asked
for the life of your enemies, but have asked for yourself
discernment to understand justice, behold, I have done
according to your words. Behold, I have given you a wise
and discerning heart, so that there has been no one like
you before you, nor shall one like you arise after you. And
I have also given you what you have not asked, both riches
and honor, so that there will not be any among the kings
like you all your days. And if you walk in My ways, keeping My statutes and commandments, as your father David
walked, then I will prolong your days."

1 Kings 3:5–14 NAS

Spend a couple of minutes with me as we ponder this
conversation between God and Solomon in its chronological
order. It is filled with a number of intriguing points of interest.

First, God opens the talk with an offer to bless Solomon in
the way of his own choosing. Today, in a similar way, God
has given each of us the opportunity to use His blessings of
life, health, and work as we wish. We can spend these blessings serving our own whims and desires and building mon-

uments and empires to ourselves, or we can reinvest them in more eternally profitable pursuits.

Next, notice King Solomon's response. It is very different from what we might expect from one of the most powerful men on the face of the earth. He begins by verbally reminding God (and himself) of his own frailty and utter dependence upon God. Here we see a king comparing himself with a weak and ignorant child! What a beautiful example of humility.

After reacquainting himself with his own unworthiness, Solomon does as God asked and makes his request. But instead of making a grab for selfish ambition, the king asks for a gift that will help him serve his people more effectively. He asks for wisdom to be a better and more righteous leader. His goal was to more effectively serve those he led.

Finally, notice what God's response was when Solomon asked for wisdom. Verse 10 tells us God found the king's request pleasing. It's not that Solomon would have been condemned if he had asked for something else. Surely God would have given it to him. But by asking for wisdom to help him serve God better, Solomon also received the blessings of riches and honor to a degree never seen before or since!

The Bottom Line

The fact is, there is only one best way to do anything. When that "best way" has been determined, the wise individual will keep doing it over and over again until it becomes a habit. Eventually, that habit will lead to achievement.

Like so many other things, effective time management is a critically important part of a disciplined life-style. It requires a balanced combination of hard work and clearheaded thinking. This hurdle has caused many would-be achievers to fail.

Testifying to this fact are the multitudes of businesses, ministries, and families that have failed because of an irresponsible work ethic. However, effective time management is a discipline that can be applied by anyone who wants to enjoy a tranquil and orderly existence. The question is this: Are you really willing to pay the price? Only *time* will tell.

Unlike some topics, there is no way to effectively discuss time management without a strong dose of self-discipline. Sometimes Christians confuse slothfulness with meekness. We tend to excuse laziness and second-rate performance rather than demand the very best from ourselves.

Christians, more than any other group, should be peak performers. We should applaud and appreciate the time and talents God has entrusted to us. We, of all people, should be the best at investing the time God has allowed us because, just as with all of His other gifts, one day God will ask for an accounting of how we redeemed the time.

"*OVER THE YEARS,
MORE FAMILIES HAVE
BEEN SAVED, MORE
WARS AVERTED,
MORE RELATIONSHIPS
FORGED
BY THOSE WITH OPEN
EARS THAN BY
THOSE WITH
OPEN MOUTHS.*"

11

THE FORGOTTEN ART OF LISTENING

There are approximately 600,000 words in the English language. Experts tells us the average American uses somewhere between 10,000 and 20,000 of these words in his or her active vocabulary. That same individual may recognize up to 20,000 more words when reading or listening. In the course of a typical day, most individuals will see, hear, and be exposed to over 1600 advertising messages. *Merchandising* magazine reports that 999 out of every 1000 American homes has at least one television set. Of course, radio is the consummate "listening" media. There are six radios in the average home in this country. Over 95 percent of our automobiles are radio equipped. There are over 500 million radios in use, with over 60 million new ones purchased each year. Every week, 95 percent of all persons twelve and over listen to the radio.

With this tremendous volume of information constantly before us, you would think we would be adept listeners.

After all, we sure get a lot of practice! However, I am convinced that a lot more is said in our society than is ever really heard. Most people function at only 25 to 30 percent of their maximum listening efficiency. One survey indicated that 40 to 60 percent of us probably cannot remember a single conversation we had with anyone yesterday. Seven days after hearing it, the average individual retains only 10 percent of a ten-minute oral presentation. Everybody's talking, but nobody seems to be listening.

In *Listening Behavior*, Larry L. Barker reports that up to 75 percent of our waking hours are spent communicating in one of four ways: listening, 42 percent of the time; talking, 32 percent of the time; reading, 15 percent of the time; and writing, 11 percent of the time. However, for most of us, school years were devoted to teaching us to read, write, and speak. It appears that something very important was left out.

One of the best ways I know to be well liked and appreciated in almost any circle is to be a good listener. I believe it was Wilson Mizner who said, "A good listener is not only popular everywhere, but after a while he knows something." Think about it: don't you enjoy being around someone who likes to listen to you? Don't you like it when someone elicits your opinions on a matter and then really listens to what you have to say?

Experts are now beginning to think that one of Ronald Reagan's keys to success was his willingness to listen. While he was in the White House, public opinion polling went on at an unprecedented level. Richard Wirthlin, President Reagan's pollster and friend, used survey research to listen to the national heartbeat. During those eight years, more than 500,000 Americans responded to more than 500 surveys. It may well be that one reason he was "The Great Communicator" was that he also was "The Great Listener."

Benjamin Franklin said it best: "A pair of good ears will drink dry a hundred tongues." People everywhere are craving someone who cares enough to listen. The problem with so many of us is that we are addicted to the sound of our own voices! We tend to ignore valid thoughts and opinions from others. We forget that it is virtually impossible to minister to someone else without first learning their needs. In an effort to serve God through glorious deeds, we overlook the mundane, simple deeds of service—deeds such as listening to someone who is weighed down with a problem.

In addition to the ministerial side of listening are some very practical, hard-nosed reasons that make being a good listener vital in the professional arena. I am convinced that a frighteningly high percentage of relational problems and confusion are directly attributable to the failure to listen carefully.

If the average individual in this nation's 100 million-person workforce made one listening mistake per week that cost his employer ten dollars, the annual cost would exceed fifty billion dollars! That's fifty billion dollars we would have to pay in the form of higher prices at the cash register—all because someone did not listen and a job had to be redone, an order was not processed, or a product was shipped to the wrong address. Imagine the even higher price we pay for not listening to our children when they need to talk with us! Think about the broken marriages and lost fellowships that have occurred because someone wasn't willing to listen to a spouse or friend! I wonder if a failure to listen hasn't even caused wars that might have been avoided.

A Simple Solution

Now that we see the problem, what is the solution? Actually, it is not a difficult solution to understand, but it is tough to apply. The solution? Learn to listen better. Sounds easy enough, but like going on a diet, it will take a change of life-style for most of us. As children, many of us grew up trying to "get a word in edgewise." It was almost a rite of passage the night we first intercepted the dinner table conversation and, like a star halfback, maintained possession of it all the way to dessert. Besides, isn't there something in the Constitution that assures us the right to talk 150 words per minute—with gusts up to 180?

We must learn to listen if we are ever going to be truly great communicators. The good news is that experts feel we can double our listening efficiency through knowledge and practice. Unlike the ability to sing, listening isn't a talent with which only a select few are born. Listening is a learned skill. Anyone can do it if he or she wants to badly enough.

The Listening Void

In their best-selling book, *In Search of Excellence*, authors Thomas J. Peters and Robert H. Waterman suggest that most American companies experience significant problems because management fails to listen attentively to customers and employees. Today's business climate is like a furnace. The pressure is intense. Most managers are so overloaded, they feel that listening to subordinates is a luxury they can't afford. Listening takes a backseat to the more aggressive forms of communication, such as giving orders.

Unfortunately, the same mistake is made in many churches. The people in the pews are sometimes ignored by the church "professionals." How sad and foreign this is to what the Lord wants. Even in the home, where we should be the most attentive to the thoughts and ideas of others, we frequently fail to even hear what is being said. Every year there are thousands of divorces because men don't listen to their wives. Every night there are kids roaming streets all over America looking for someone who cares—someone who will simply listen to what they have to say.

A Costly Listening Error

We have experienced this same problem in our firm. Far too often, I have heard myself talking when I should have been listening. Deadlines have been missed when people in the creative department didn't listen to the account executive's instructions. Upon occasion, we have had to rework a project because of a listening deficiency. Few things annoy me more than having to redesign an ad or reprint a corporate brochure because I failed to listen to the client's directions at the beginning of the project.

We are aware of this problem, and we have taken at least one step to help remedy it. Ours may be the only advertising agency in America that doesn't have a conference room. That's right—no conference room. We do have a room that has a big table, a bunch of chairs, media presentation equipment, and awards on the walls. This may sound like a conference room, but it's not.

Instead of a conference room, we have a "Listening Room." That's what the brass plate on the door says, and that's exactly what it is: a room where we come to listen attentively. That little brass plate helps us remember that we will never be able to serve our clients adequately until we have first listened to them and learned their needs.

Now this seems like a simple concept. No one would put up with a doctor who grabbed him the moment he walked into the office, anesthetized him, and began surgery—all without discussing the patient's symptoms first. Yet it takes a conscious effort for me not to do that very thing with my clients and co-workers. It is my tendency to talk first and think later.

I recently had a very sobering experience. Our company had made a presentation to an architectural firm in hopes of winning its account. It was a project we really wanted to win. Several weeks passed, and we received no word on whether or not we would get the business. Finally, I called one of the principals to ask if they had made a decision.

"Yes," he told me, "we have. We've decided not to do anything at this point. I could make up some sort of excuse, but instead I want to tell you why we aren't going to proceed with the project. It's because we don't think you ever really learned enough about our business. You never asked enough questions. When we tried to tell you about our needs—you didn't listen."

Ouch! That hurt. But their assessment probably held a lot of truth. I had really blown it. My failure to listen had caused embarrassment and financial loss.

A Listening Exercise

As is the case with any other bad habit, it takes a little effort and self-discipline to overcome this problem. It means paying more attention to the way we communicate with others. Sometimes we'll have to bite our tongues and open our ears. If you are like me and tend to talk too much and listen too little, you may want to try this little developmental exercise the next time you are in a conference or listening situation:

1. If you are not expected to direct the meeting or speak on an expert level, make it a point not to be the first to speak. If no one else speaks, you may wish to break the ice, but do so by introducing someone else into the conversation and encouraging his or her comments. Then be quiet and listen.

2. While it is not always practical, try not to speak until everyone else has spoken and someone in the meeting solicits your input. This is beneficial on at least two levels: First, the credibility of what you say is heightened when someone else elicits your thoughts and sits prepared to listen. Often the people who voluntarily talk the most enjoy the least respect from their peers. Second, you can now make all of your observations based on information gained from the others' comments. This can save you from making comments based on incomplete data and incorrect assumptions.

*3. While someone else is speaking, make a conscious effort to **really** listen.* Don't allow yourself to become preoccupied by peripheral distractions. If you begin thinking about the room temperature, the art on the walls, or other things, you'll leave the discussion not knowing what was said. Make it a point to look at the speaker. Don't rattle your change, play with your pen, or make a little paper airplane out of her business card.

Concentrate on what the speaker is actually saying—not what you *think* she's saying. Often, listeners hear only the first few words of a sentence, finish it with their own thoughts—and miss the speaker's actual comments.

Avoid paying too much attention to what the speaker is wearing or whether he is too fat or she's too tall. Remember, your purpose for being there isn't to make a visual analysis of the speaker's grooming or wardrobe. The average person speaks about 125 words per minute. It is thought that the average listener can comprehend between 400 and 600 words per minute. Thus, a listener has about 75 percent of his time free. He can use this time either to allow his thoughts to wander or to absorb and process what is being communicated. When the listener does the latter, he can significantly improve his long-term recall.

4. *It is entirely appropriate to assess the speaker on his or her body language.* As you listen to the speaker's words, learn to study his facial expressions and the way he holds himself. Look for messages within the message. Any student of people can learn to spot the telltale signs of a person who feels uncomfortable with what he is saying. This discomfort may be simply because he's nervous, or it may be an indication of doubt, incompetence, or a low credibility level. Often, when you are in a communicative situation, the other person's body language will tell you whether he is receptive to your thoughts and ideas or whether it is best to step away and pick up at another time and place.

One word of caution here: It is true that facial expressions, voice tone, gestures, and body positions frequently are indications of a person's actual feelings. However, it normally requires a cluster of these various expressions to indicate a true attitude or thought. Don't be in too big a hurry to assume someone dislikes you just because he crosses his arms. He might just be trying to hide a missing button.

5. *Make it a point to take notes as the other people talk.* If you arrive at a business meeting without a yellow legal pad and a pen, you are not prepared for that meeting. Taking notes helps in several ways. First, it tells your co-workers that what they have to say *is* important to you. Once they understand that you are taking their comments seriously, they will tend to make a better presentation. Second, it will help you remember and respond to important points that are made. Third, it is a scientific fact that you cannot take notes and talk simultaneously. In other words, if you tend to dominate the conversation, get busy writing notes!

6. Be a friendly listener. Try to maintain an interested, pleasant face as you watch the speaker. This will tend to put him at ease and allow him to make a more informative presentation.

7. When you do speak, show a sincere interest in what your peers have presented. The people before you have thoughts, feelings, loves, and hurts. They are flesh and blood. They all have immortal souls. They deserve your deepest care and compassion. Jesus always spoke words that were seasoned with grace and love. Should we do any less?

As Christian leaders, we should communicate God's grace whenever and wherever we speak. It should be our goal to put others at ease. We should leave others feeling better when we finish our comments than they did before we started. This attitude can be communicated in a number of ways.

It is always good to begin by making a positive response to what has just been said. If you have points of agreement with the speaker, say so. It can also be helpful to preface your comments with questions directed to those who have just spoken regarding what they said. Don't hesitate to ask for clarification or more information. Attempt to make your questions as penetrating and insightful as possible. If this doesn't come easy for you, listen to the way small children ask questions. Kids have a way of asking questions that could baffle Solomon. One day, when Joshua was about three, he strolled up to me and said, "Daddy, how do bones get inside of people?" I'm still working on that one.

One of the most successful employees I've ever had is a marathon question asker. After he first started with us, we almost dreaded seeing him in the hall because he always had another fifty questions to ask. One day he told me he figured he could gain three or four years of experience within a few months if he asked enough questions. Within less than half a year, he was a top account executive.

One of the best ways we can maximize our effectiveness and become appreciated by those around us is by being good, caring listeners. Although the talent is underrated and undervalued, those who learn to listen effectively will have a real tool with which to better serve others. Yet, like any other discipline, listening takes practice and concentration. It is a learned skill.

As a general rule, we would be wise to apply the 70/30 rule: Listen 70 percent of the time, and speak no more than 30 percent of the time. This very closely approximates the 2-to-1 ratio that already exists between the number of ears and mouths with which we come equipped.

"*AND IT IS HE WHO WILL GO AS A FORERUNNER BEFORE HIM IN THE SPIRIT AND POWER OF ELIJAH, TO TURN THE HEARTS OF THE FATHERS BACK TO THE CHILDREN, AND THE DISOBEDIENT TO THE ATTITUDE OF THE RIGHTEOUS; SO AS TO MAKE READY A PEOPLE PREPARED FOR THE LORD.*"

—*LUKE 1:17 NAS*

12

KEEPING THE HOME FIRES BURNING

I'm beginning this last chapter in a room at Baptist Hospital in downtown Nashville. Bonnie and I are about to have our fourth baby. All morning there have been nurses, attendants, and a doctor helping Bonnie prepare for the new arrival. Things are hectic. Everyone is busy performing his or her individual tasks. What interests me most is the way everyone has been so devoted to the needs of Bonnie and the baby. Nothing has been left undone. Nothing is left to guesswork. Everyone is intent on reducing the chance of a problem. No one wants a complication. Blood tests, shots, monitors—every precaution is taken.

Since Bonnie must have a cesarean section, things will be a bit more complicated. The anesthesiologist came in earlier. He spent half an hour discussing the various procedures and recommended the one he felt would be the safest. As he spoke to us, it became evident that he was a Christian. As a final preparatory step, he led us all in a prayer before leaving the room. Everyone has gone out of their way to make certain this will be a successful birth.

Things are moving along briskly now. Bonnie was just taken down the hall, where she will be prepared for the actual surgical procedure. One of the nurses brought me a sterile gown to wear in the operating room. It is obvious that I wouldn't be allowed into that sanitary atmosphere wearing my street clothes. As a matter of fact, I've even been supplied with coverings for my shoes. No detail has been overlooked. Clearly, everyone involved in this project is going to be clean, scrubbed, and ready for the job in front of them.

The real question is, will we remain as careful with this child's ongoing nurturing as we are about the birth? Will we monitor his or her activities? Will we study behavior patterns and react promptly if there is a glitch on the screen? Will we pray daily that this little one stands upright before God? Are we going to take his or her spiritual health seriously? Will we deal with this child with clean hands? Will this new life receive regular checkups by the Great Physician?

So often, we pay a lot of attention to the physical side and virtually ignore the spiritual. I hope we will teach this little person what success is really all about. More precisely, as the father and head of this home, I hope I'll take my job seriously.

What exactly is my job? It is to deliver this new child back to God with a clean and righteous heart.

Today, in the midst of all the emotions, I feel very dependent upon God. I am intensely aware of my need for Him. But, assuming everything goes smoothly here today, will I forget my desperate need for God tomorrow, next month, or next year? Will I slowly but surely slip my hand out of God's hand as if to say, "Thanks for the help, but now I'll handle this child on my own"?

Today we are beginning a marathon race, not a fifty-yard dash. Are we going to trust God to help us go the distance? I hope so.

Remembering Where the Front Line Is Located

If he wants to win the battle, one thing a general has to remember is the location of the front line. If he doesn't know where the front line is, he is likely to deploy troops where they aren't needed. Worse, he might not deploy enough troops where the battle is the most fierce. He may route supplies to nonessential areas. In short, he could cost his troops the victory.

All too often, men confuse the important with the urgent. Business magazines are running more and more articles on the workaholic phenomenon. Researchers are beginning to suggest that many of us who belong to the baby boom generation are shaping up as great businessmen but very poor husbands and fathers. In an effort to get ahead (whatever that means), families are often deserted by dads who spend far too much time at the office and in nightly meetings.

Sometimes we forget where our front line is located. We allow job pressures to claim far too many of our hours. Nighttime business calls steal precious family time that can never be replaced. Board meetings and overnight business trips tend to make us strangers in our own homes.

Yet it is in the home where our true success or failure will be measured. The home is the primary arena in which we must succeed if we are to be successful in any of the others. The problem is that it is hard to have a storybook, Brady Bunch family when we are going 100 miles per hour—usually in different directions. We are so loaded with piano lessons, baseball practice, gymnastics, art classes, and church work that we rarely see one another, except in the car. The years pass at breakneck speed, and we don't realize what we've missed until it's too late.

A Return to My Senses

I'll never forget a white water rafting trip Bonnie and I took down the Ocoee River a few years ago. We had enjoyed a wonderful day of family activities before the trip. With the children and grandparents taking the car to the end of the run, Bonnie, three others, and I launched the raft.

The trip went flawlessly until the very last rapid. This particular portion of the trip is considered the most treacherous because the rapid is located immediately below a bridge. The object is to navigate the raft through the whirlpools without getting too close to a bridge pylon. That particular day, something went wrong and the raft got into the wrong place. Suddenly, a day of family fun turned into a nightmare. Before we knew what was happening, we were being swept off course into the very bridge pylon we most wanted to avoid! With thousands of tons of water pressure coming down on us, the raft immediately wrapped itself around the pylon. As I reached for Bonnie, a wave washed me out of the raft and through the whirlpool.

A few minutes later, I shot out of the rapid and washed up several hundred feet downstream. Like a dagger, it suddenly hit me: *Where's Bonnie?* Frantically, I rushed up the bank, making my way through the undergrowth to the main road, and headed back upstream.

Reaching the bridge, I looked down to the pylon where our raft had been. By this time, the water pressure had caused it to burst like a balloon at a child's birthday party. What remained looked like a giant piece of blue bubble gum wrapped around the pylon. It was being held there by the sheer force of the rushing water. Standing on top of the exploded raft, clinging to the bridge pylon with the water only inches below their feet, were three desperate people. Everyone was there—except Bonnie!

In those next few heart-stopping moments, I rushed across the bridge until I was directly above the disaster. Leaning over the rail and looking straight down, I saw what I'd been unable to see from shore. It was my best friend! She was still there, clinging to the back side of the pylon.

The next few minutes were a blur. Several of us quickly devised a plan to lower a lifeline and harness each individual to safety. I'll never forget how good it was to see Bonnie finally reach the bridge!

I nearly lost my wife on that trip. That day my feelings for Bonnie were intense. I felt my love for her in an unusually profound way. I would have done anything for her that day. The problem is, those emotions soon wore off. Things went back to the normal and mundane. That highly charged surge of love I had felt for Bonnie immediately after the accident soon gave way to the same selfishness I had exhibited previously.

Living in the Common World

The fact is, there aren't going to be many of those high-voltage occurrences for most of us. The challenge is to find our contentment and happiness—our success—in the common world. It's a matter of making the common moments count, and for most of us, that's not easy. Frequently, we allow the abundance of the average to destroy our most important relationship: our family.

As I mentioned in an earlier chapter, the person who becomes financially successful usually does so by finding something he or she can do commercially and then doing that same thing over and over until one day he wakes up to realize he has made a lot of money. Unfortunately, the converse is true as well. The reason many would-be entrepreneurs fail in the financial realm is that they jump from one get-rich-quick scheme to another. They never learn to persevere at anything long enough to succeed.

This same problem occurs in the home. Hollywood has conditioned us to expect every day in the life of a married couple to be filled with glib one-liners and no health or financial concerns that can't be solved between commercial breaks. Real life just isn't that way. The real world includes real hurt and real pain.

The Squirm Factor

Today, many people are looking for what I call "squirming area." They don't like the idea of making an airtight commitment. When the going gets tough, they get going—in the other direction. This is the reason for so many of the divorces in America. The divorce rate in the United States has risen from about 150 per 1000 marriages before World War II to 500 per 1000 marriages in the mid-1970s. And what happens to the children? The Census Bureau estimates that about 60 percent of all children born in the late 1980s will spend some time living in a single-parent home.

However, if divorce has lost its stigma, it still hasn't lost its sting. One little boy put it this way: "I feel like a Ping-Pong ball going back and forth between my mom and dad." A teenager described divorce this way: "Divorce. It stinks. The only difference in our home now is we don't have as much yelling. It's just quiet. But you know something? I preferred the yelling."

I am convinced that there is no such thing as a truly successful person who has failed with his family. Success at home comes when we learn to follow the advice of the Apostle Peter:

> You husbands likewise, live with your wives *in an understanding way*, as with a weaker vessel, since she is a woman; and *grant her honor* as a fellow-heir of the grace of life, so that your prayers may not be hindered. To sum up, let all be harmonious, sympathetic, brotherly, kindhearted, and humble in spirit; not returning evil for evil, or insult for insult, but giving a blessing instead; for you were called for the very purpose that you might inherit a blessing.
>
> 1 Peter 3:7–9 NAS, my italics

In my Bible, I have two phrases underlined in this passage: *in an understanding way* and *grant her honor*. It's not that I've accomplished these two goals. To the contrary, I'm a miserable failure much of the time. But it is my aim to constantly improve in my methods of dealing with Bonnie. I want to show her the understanding and respect she needs and deserves. Why? Well, obviously because God tells me to do so, and also because it will make my wife a happier person. But there's another reason for me to take this direction from Peter seriously. Did you notice the last part of the passage? Peter makes an interesting comment: ". . . for the very purpose that you might inherit a blessing." I wonder what he means by that. Do you suppose there could be a blessing from God for those husbands who really do understand and honor their wives? I believe so.

Considering the Children

Fathers, the most important gift you can give your children is to love their mother. I am convinced that Daddy should love Mom more than anyone else—including the children.

One night at dinner, I was taken aback when Joshua (who was five at the time) stopped eating, looked at me, and asked, "You love Mama more than you love us, don't you, Daddy?"

His question caught me off guard and I didn't know what to say. But his older sister, Megan, spoke very matter-of-factly between bites: "Sure he does." That ended that. I realized our children derive much of their stability from knowing their Mom and Dad are each other's best friends.

I guess this pretty much brings us full cycle. We began this book by suggesting that God's concept of success is very different from the world's concept of success. As we have gone along, I have attempted to share some of the characteristics of godly success and how to enjoy it. Hopefully, we have been able to see a clear difference between God's ways and the world's ways.

In this concluding chapter, we have zeroed in on what I believe is the most fundamental arena in which to succeed: the home. As I explained, this issue is an especially poignant one as we witness the birth of our fourth child. I began by sharing some of my personal concerns with you. Will this new infant see Jesus living in me? Will Bonnie and I be successful in training this child to know and love God? Will this young person succeed in the eyes of God and one day receive His eternal reward?

In Deuteronomy 6:6–9 NAS, God speaks directly to parents concerning this issue:

> And these words, which I am commanding you today, shall be on your heart; and you shall teach them diligently to your sons and shall talk of them when you sit in your house and when you walk by the way and when you lie down and when you rise up. And you shall bind them as a sign on your hand and they shall be as frontals on your forehead. And you shall write them on the doorposts of your house and on your gates.

For me, ultimate success will come the day each member of our family stands redeemed before God and hears Him say:

> Well done, good and faithful servant; you have been faithful over a little, I will set you over much; enter into the joy of your master.
>
> Matthew 25:21 RSV

By the way, Mary Grace weighed in at 7 pounds, 5½ ounces.

STUDY QUESTIONS

1 Square Pegs and Round Holes

1. What biblical examples show a situation where two people had very different perspectives? Read the following verses and write a description of the characters and each one's perspective.

   a. Genesis 4:3–5, 7

   b. Genesis 13:10–13

2. If the following statement is true, "God has engineered, designed, and built each one of us with a set of characteristics and abilities that He expects to be used to His glory" then list what you consider are those characteristics and abilities you have been given. Describe how each of these abilities can be used and viewed from the two perspectives mentioned above. Consider which perspective you've used with your abilities so far.

3. Look up 1 Samuel 17 and Romans 15:20–24. What was man's plan? What was God's plan? Are there circumstances in your life where your actions are more your plan than God's plan?

4. Read 1 Corinthians 12:14–21. What part of the body are you? If you are not sure, how do you think you can find out?

5. Stepping out in a new direction can be scary. List examples of people in Scripture who have stepped out into the unknown in faith. (A few examples among many are found in Genesis 12:1–3, Exodus 3 and Matthew 14:22–33.)

6. Saul is the perfect example of a person who "did it his way." What "success" did Saul have in the world's eye? What did Saul lack to be "successful" in God's eyes? (Read 1 Samuel 8–11, 13:1–15, and 15.)

7. What is one concrete step you can take today to help you on the path toward success in God's eyes? Be specific.

2 Two Great Secrets of Successful People

1. Examine the "hole in your heart." What have you tried to fill that hole with in the past? Has it been successful?

2. If God does speak to us in three ways, how has God spoken to you?
   a. Through the Bible
   b. Through people
   c. Through circumstances

3. Can you name any biblical characters who were given guidance through one or more of these three ways? (A few examples among many are found in Acts 8:26–39, Nehemiah 1, and 2 Samuel 12:1–14.)

4. Are there examples from your life where you pushed ahead to your own detriment, before seeking God's will?

5. In 1 Corinthians 2:10–15 Paul talks about being "taught by the Spirit, combining spiritual thoughts with spiritual words." What do you think that means?

3 Racing with the Rats

1. Read the parable in Luke 10:25–37. List the excuses used by those who passed by the wounded man. Have you heard or used excuses like this recently?
2. Search your own soul and list how you think you are a positive influence on the people with whom you come into contact. Use specific examples.
3. How are you a negative influence on the people with whom you come into contact? Use specific examples.
4. What biblical examples can you think of who were like the rat who "bumps his nose through a trial-and-error existence?" (A few examples among many are found in Matthew 26:33–35, 69–75, John 18:10, 11, Judges 16:15–31, and Genesis 32:22–32.)
5. What is your mental attitude toward the trials and tribulations in your life? Are you allowing God to work or are you operating by trial and error? What concrete step can you take today that will help you avoid banging your head against the wall and direct you toward "success" in God's eyes?

4 Bill, the Word Is Integrity

1. In the everyday world of integrity, how would you grade yourself? Do you believe your reputation is as a person who keeps his or her word, or do you think others see you as being deficient in integrity?
2. What biblical examples can you think of who showed an "integrity deficit of deceit?" How did their deceit change their

lives? (A few examples among many are found in Acts 5:1–6, Matthew 26:47–50, and 2 Samuel 11.)

3. Making the right choices is not always easy. Scripture gives many instances of individuals who struggled with making the choice between right or wrong action. Look up the following verses and describe the situation and the person's choices.
   a. Matthew 4:1–11
   b. Genesis 3:1–6
   c. John 13:2

4. Since we all have made wrong choices, how do we go about correcting those wrongs? Read the following verses and see if they apply specifically to any situation in your own life: Mark 6:12, Matthew 3:8, and 1 John 1:9.

5 Self-Confidence: A Christian Perspective

1. Read Genesis 3:1–7 and answer the following:
   a. How did Satan question God's authority?
   b. What was the source of Eve's self-confidence?
   c. What was the outcome of this self-confidence?
   d. How does Eve's self-confidence of Genesis 3:6 differ from Paul's self-confidence of Philippians 4:13?
   e. Is the root of your own self-confidence (or lack of it) based on the same source as Eve's self-confidence? Or do you have the same source of self-confidence as Paul?

2. If you struggle with the sin of pride, the following verses may prove helpful—Hosea 10:13–15, Daniel 5:22–30 and 2 Samuel 15–18—especially 15:4 and 18:18. At the same time, take comfort because God can restore you as evidenced in Daniel 5:18–21.

3. What positive actions can you take to express your self-confidence through Christ and not through your own actions?

Be specific; it is often easy to talk about change but more difficult to take concrete steps to make it happen.

6 The Importance of Being Likable

1. Using the description in this chapter of the two ways of gaining influence, note the following biblical examples of characters who gained influence. Note which of the two ways they used to gain that influence:
   a. Joseph (see Genesis 39, 40, 41)
   b. Daniel (see Daniel 1)
   c. Absalom (see 2 Samuel 15)
   d. Eli's sons (see 1 Samuel 2:12–36)
   e. Moses (see Exodus 3 and 4)
2. How does Nehemiah show the four characteristics of servant leadership? Read Nehemiah 1–4 and explain how Nehemiah:
   a. Developed goals that benefited those who followed him
   b. Was willing to roll up his sleeves and get involved
   c. Had a high level of God-oriented confidence
   d. Was enthusiastic with an eye toward the eternal
3. What immediate steps can you take in your own life to make each one of the four characteristics more evident? Be specific.

7 Learning to Give It Back

1. Read "The Sheep and the Goats" in Matthew 25:31–46 and answer the following questions:
   a. In your family, neighborhood, and community, what are some specific and practical ways you could "feed the hungry?"
   b. In your family, neighborhood, and community, what are some specific and practical ways you could "invite a stranger in?"

    c. In your family, neighborhood, and community, what are some specific and practical ways you could "clothe those without clothes?"

    d. In your family, neighborhood, and community, what are some specific and practical ways you could "visit people in prison?"

    e. In your family, neighborhood, and community, what are some specific and practical ways you could "care for the sick?"

2. Several biblical characters had questions and/or problems concerning money. Look up Matthew 22:15–22, Acts 5:1–10, and 1 Kings 17:7–24. List the characters and what you think the lesson was they were being taught.

3. Look up Malachi 3:8–12 and identify what was pointed out to you in this chapter—what God guarantees, what God protects, and what God will do on a national level if we give Him what is His due.

4. Are you giving God all He is due? If not, what concrete action can you take to improve matters?

8 The Positive Affirmation

1. Is "Positive Affirmation" biblical? Look up the following verses, all written by the same man, all affirming himself in a positive way before God and others.* What is he affirming about himself in each of these verses?

    a. 2 Timothy 4:7

    b. Romans 9:1

    c. Philippians 4:13

    d. Philippians 3:12

    e. 2 Corinthians 12:10

*In this individual's life, he was honest and also freely discussed his faults, but the principle of positive affirmation in motivating himself and others was quite evident in his life.

2. Start your positive affirmation list. Think through your own life and list those areas that could be positive affirmations to you:
   a.
   b.
   c.
   d.
   e.
   f.
3. In what concrete ways can you show "positive affirmation" to the following:
   a. Family
   b. Church
   c. Work

9 Building Memories

1. Building memories is God-ordained. Just look up the following verses (only a few of the many) and list the circumstances, how a memory was being built, and what was to be remembered:
   a. Genesis 9:12–16
   b. Genesis 28:10–22
   c. Exodus 28:21
   d. Deuteronomy 10:1–10
   e. Joshua 4:3
2. Specifically, what can you do to start building the kind of memories discussed in this chapter?
   a. In your family
   b. With your friends
   c. At work
3. What kind of memory did Paul have of the Philippians (see Philippians 1:3–6)? Are there those who would say the same

thing about you? In what ways can you begin to help others build positive memories about you?

10 Managing Your Vanishing Inventory

1. Describe how you think the verses below relate to the thoughts in this chapter.
   a. Proverbs 10:4–5
   b. Proverbs 21:5
   c. Galatians 3:3
   d. Philippians 3:14
   e. Jeremiah 17:7
2. In what areas of your life is it possible for you to work harder? In the areas listed, note specific actions you need to take this week.
3. In what areas of your life is it possible for you to work smarter? In the areas listed, note specific actions you need to take this week.
4. If you've had time to ponder, pray, and meditate concerning your long-term goals, state those goals here.

11 The Forgotten Art of Listening

1. Read the story of the young Samuel and note what one can learn about listening and the hindrances to listening (1 Samuel 3).
2. Note what each of the following verses has to do with the content of this chapter, "The Forgotten Art of Listening."
   a. Proverbs 12:15
   b. Proverbs 18:13
   c. Proverbs 19:20
   d. Proverbs 20:18
   e. Psalm 46:10

3. Note the specific actions you can take to become a better listener in the following:
   a. Home
   b. Among friends
   c. Work

12 Keeping the Home Fires Burning

1. We know more about David than any other person in Scripture except for Christ. Look up the following verses and note the positive or negative aspect of David as father:
   a. 2 Samuel 12:15–20
   b. 2 Samuel 13:37
   c. 2 Samuel 18:5
   d. 1 Kings 2:1–4
2. What can we learn in the Prodigal Son story (Luke 15:11–32) about the characteristics of a good father? List them.
3. What are specific steps you can take with your children this week to help you in "Keeping the Home Fires Burning?"
4. Read Ephesians 5:25–33 and list the ways you can begin to take to help you love your wife "as Christ loves the Church." Be specific, not philosophical.

BIBLIOGRAPHY

To one degree or another, I have formed some of my thoughts from the following books, as well as scores of other books, articles, and life experiences. But the one book that is must reading for anyone who is dedicated to achieving and enjoying godly success is the Holy Bible. Read it. Study it. Live it. Then you will know success that is success indeed.

Ailes, Roger, with Jon Krausher. *You Are the Message*. Homewood, Illinois: Dow Jones-Irwin, 1988.

Allen, James. *As a Man Thinketh*. New York: Gosset & Dunlap, distributed by the Putnam Publishing Group, 1984.

Blanchard, Kenneth, and Norman Vincent Peale. *The Power of Ethical Management*. New York: William Morrow & Company, 1988.

Burkett, Larry. *Answers to Your Family's Financial Questions*. Pomona, California: Focus on the Family Publications, 1987.

Crabb, Lawrence J., Jr., and Dan B. Allender. *Encouragement, The Key to Caring*. Grand Rapids, Michigan: Pyranee Books, 1984.

Dobson, Dr. James. *Love Must Be Tough.* Waco, Texas: Word Books, 1983.

Erwin, Gayle D. *The Jesus Style.* Waco, Texas: Word Books, 1983.

Foster, Richard J. *Money, Sex, and Power.* New York: Harper & Row, Publishers, 1985.

Hazelip, Harold, and Ken Durham. *Becoming Persons of Integrity.* Grand Rapids, Michigan: Baker Book House, 1988.

Hemfelt, Dr. Robert, Dr. Frank Minirth, and Dr. Paul Meier. *Love Is a Choice.* Nashville: Thomas Nelson Publishers, 1989.

Morley, Patrick M. *The Man in the Mirror.* Brentwood, Tennessee: Wolgemuth & Hyatt Publishers, 1989.

Peters, Thomas J., and Robert H. Waterman. *In Search of Excellence.* New York: Warner Books, 1984.

Rush, Myron. *Lord of the Marketplace.* Wheaton, Illinois: Victor Books, 1986.

Shelly, Rubel. *The Beatitudes: Jesus' Formula for Happiness.* Nashville: Twentieth Century Christian, 1982, 1984.

Smalley, Gary, and John Trent, Ph.D. *The Blessing.* Nashville: Thomas Nelson Publishers, 1986.

Sherman, Doug, and William Hendricks. *How to Succeed Where It Really Counts.* Colorado Springs, Colorado: Navpress, 1989.

Ziglar, Zig. *See You at the Top.* Gretna, Louisiana: Pelican Publishing Company, 1983.

LaVergne, TN USA
14 March 2011
219998LV00003B/1/P